THE INDUSTRIAL REVOLUTION
IN COVENTRY

THE
INDUSTRIAL REVOLUTION
IN COVENTRY

by

JOHN PREST

Fellow of Balliol College, Oxford

OXFORD UNIVERSITY PRESS

1960

Oxford University Press, Amen House, London E.C.4

GLASGOW   NEW YORK   TORONTO   MELBOURNE   WELLINGTON
BOMBAY   CALCUTTA   MADRAS   KARACHI   KUALA LUMPUR
CAPE TOWN   IBADAN   NAIROBI   ACCRA

*Printed in Great Britain by
The Camelot Press Ltd., London and Southampton*

PREFACE

I am most grateful to Miss D. A. Leech and to her assistant in the Coventry City Record Office, Mr. Denton, who have taken great trouble to help me; to Miss Alice Lynes, who has put all the resources of the Coventry and Warwickshire Collection at my disposal; to Mr. Edgar Letts, who has given me the run of the files of the *Coventry Standard*; to Miss Joan Lancaster and Mrs. Tomlinson, both working for the Victoria County History, who have helped me with population problems and 'topshops' respectively; to Mrs. Fretton, Mr. S. Alexander, and Mr. A. W. Treharn for advice about the watch trade; to Messrs. Cash, Messrs. Oakey & Cox, and Mr. Walter Dunn for advice about the ribbon trade; to Mr. S. Alexander, Messrs. Cash, Messrs. Oakey & Cox, Messrs. Liggins & Son, and Mr. P. Avery all of whom have allowed me to make plans of their houses; to Miss Jane Millerchip, Mr. R. J. Buckingham, Mr. Edgar Letts, and A. H. Gardner and partners, who have given me introductions; to Mr. W. F. Holmes and Mr. J. E. Cruickshank, who have taken photographs for me; to Mrs. R. J. Buckingham and Dr. Margaret Cruickshank, who have so kindly put me up on my many visits to Coventry; to Miss D. A. Leech, Miss Alice Lynes, Mr. Denton, Mr. A. B. Hibbert, Mr. F. M. Bannister, Mr. A. B. Rodger, Mr. R. W. Southern, and Dr. R. M. Hartwell who have read all or part of the text; and to Miss A. Dodd and Mrs. Jayakar who typed it.

J. M. P.

CONTENTS

INTRODUCTION   ix

I. FOUR OF THE PEOPLE OF COVENTRY   1

II. THE CITY AND ITS POLITICS   19

III. THE ORGANIZATION OF THE RIBBON
    TRADE IN THE 1830's   43

IV. THE WAGES AND STANDARDS OF LIVING
    OF THE DIFFERENT CLASSES OF
    RIBBON WEAVERS   64

V. THE TRANSFORMATION OF THE RIBBON
    TRADE IN THE 1840's AND 1850's   79

VI. THE COTTAGE FACTORY   96

VII. THE STRUGGLE BETWEEN THE COTTAGE
    FACTORY AND THE FACTORY, AND
    THE DISASTER OF 1860   113

EPILOGUE   137

APPENDIX—THE HISTORICAL VALUE OF
    MIDDLEMARCH   143

INDEX   147

LIST OF FIGURES

1. Coventry and the weaving area   2
2. Coventry, showing the area remaining to the city after the boundary changes following the reform of the municipal corporations in 1835   22
3. The old city: detail, showing individual houses   27
4. 20 Castle Street, Hillfields: a two story weaver's house   74
5. 11 Vernon Street, Hillfields: a three story weaver's house   74
6. 34 Craven Street, Chapelfields: a journeyman watchmaker's house   82
7. 32 Queen Street, Hillfields: a small ribbon-manufacturer's house   84
8. 61 Allesley Old Road, Chapelfields: a master watch-manufacturer's house   86
9. Hillfields in 1851, showing streets and the extent of building, but not individual houses   100
10. Eli Green's sixty-seven cottage factories in Hillfields   103
11. John and Joseph Cash's 'hundred' houses in Kingfield   105

LIST OF PLATES

1. 1a, Charles Bray (*Copyright Coventry Corporation*). 1b, Joseph Gutteridge   *facing p.* 14
2. Two and three story weavers' houses in Brook Street, Hillfields   *facing p.* 74
3. 34 Craven Street, Chapelfields: a journeyman watchmaker's house: front and back   *facing p.* 80
4. 61 Allesley Old Road, Chapelfields: a master watch-manufacturer's house   *facing p.* 81
5. 5a, Part of Eli Green's sixty-seven cottage factories in Hillfields. 5b, Three of John and Joseph Cash's 'hundred' houses in Kingfield   *facing p.* 106

INTRODUCTION

ENOUGH is known of four of the people of Coventry who wrote about their city in this period to make it worth saying something about them. These four are introduced in the first chapter, and their words will be found thereafter throughout the book. The most famous of the four is George Eliot, whose novels were written with an eye on the past. George Eliot understood the extent to which the lives of individual men and women were influenced by their neighbours, by their material circumstances, by events beyond their control, and even by events of which they had no knowledge.

In 1830 Coventry was a closely built town of 27,000 inhabitants, most of whom earned their living making silk ribbons or watches in their own homes. George Eliot knew that the changes which took place in this period in the working lives of the weavers of Coventry could not be considered apart from the general circumstances of the city. The second chapter, therefore, describes the state of the city in the 1830's, and touches in outline on the major physical and political changes in the period 1830-65.

In 1830 Coventry was still encircled by pasture lands which could not be enclosed without an Act of Parliament that the politics of the town made it impossible to obtain. The city was unable to expand, and provided ideal conditions for the survival of old trade customs. It is not surprising, therefore, that Coventry had fallen behind the times, and that the organization of the silk ribbon weaving, which is described in Chapter III, remained more characteristic of the eighteenth than of the nineteenth century. The dominant feature of the trade was that wages were still paid according to an agreed 'list of prices', which, if it was not legally enforceable, was nevertheless imposed by public opinion on both masters and men. The ideas behind the list were that surplus labour should not be the means of lowering wages, and that the weaver in work should receive a living wage. The meaning of this last phrase is considered in Chapter IV, which describes the wages and standards of living of the different classes of weavers.

The payment of wages according to an agreed list of prices was always under attack, and the attacks upon the list gradually gathered weight throughout the 1840's and 1850's. Technical improvements, competition from other towns, changes in the circumstances of the city and the beliefs of its inhabitants, and the actions of the government at Westminster in opening the whole trade to competition from abroad, all contributed to the course of the industrial revolution which is described in the last three chapters. While a new generation of masters broke through tradition and began to weave ribbons by power and to employ the lower class of weavers in factories, the conservatism of the better class of weavers led to the establishment of 'cottage factories', where the weavers worked by power in their own houses. These cottage factories were constructed in Coventry on a scale unequalled elsewhere.

The struggle between the factory and the cottage factory came to a head when the Anglo-French Treaty of 1860 allowed French ribbons to be imported free of duty, and culminated in the collapse of the trade, the abandonment of the list of prices, the ruin of the cottage factories, and the emigration of many weavers. The 40,000 people living in Coventry in 1865, broken by the lean years of unemployment and under-employment since 1860, were more amenable to the disciplines of nineteenth century industry—factory labour, regular hours, and the competition for work. The first stage of the upheaval by which Coventry became an engineering city had been accomplished. For the first time capital began to come to Coventry because labour was cheap. The watch trade provided the nucleus of skilled, and the ribbon trade the pool of unskilled labour, with which Coventry, graduating through the sewing-machine and the bicycle to the motor bicycle and the motor car, climbed back towards prosperity as the nineteenth century drew to its close.

Trivial as the study of a single town over so short a period may seem, there is here a contribution, however meagre, to both urban and industrial history. In 1830 Coventry still epitomized the old order, in which there were many ranks and conditions of men within a single, homogeneous society. But Coventry could not stand still while England moved, and in the end Coventry succumbed to the standards of the nineteenth century all the more painfully for her long resistance to them. By 1865 the old, compact, ordered society of 1830 had broken up: in its place were the pieces, labelled capital and labour. There was an increased awareness of class, less deference to birth, and business was conducted on the principle of individual interest without reference to the feelings of the community.

FOUR OF THE PEOPLE OF COVENTRY

FOUR of the people of Coventry have left particularly valuable evidence of their city in this period. All four were typical of their age: George Eliot, who could love mankind with saintly fervour and muster only human scepticism for God; Charles Bray, a ribbon manufacturer who neglected his trade for philosophy; Joseph Gutteridge, a weaver, and the very pattern of a Liberal working man; and William Andrews, a self-made and self-satisfied man who started work as an apprentice, and rose to be a master and an alderman.

GEORGE ELIOT

George Eliot came from the part of North Warwickshire between Coventry and Nuneaton which has always been dependent upon Coventry, and upon which alone, by the early nineteenth century, was founded Coventry's claim to be a provincial centre (see figure 1). Her father, Robert Evans, was the estate manager at Arbury, where the plain, well-timbered Midland countryside concealed the rich coal beneath. The coal was sent away in both directions along the Coventry and Oxford Canal. The colliers worked for the county landowners, while their wives and daughters worked at the ribbon weaving for the city manufacturers. The agricultural land supported clean and decent villages: the mining and weaving dirty, squalid ones. Here, indeed, within a few miles of Arbury, was the contrast described by the traveller in the introduction to *Felix Holt*, between the 'district of clean little market towns without manufactures, of fat livings, an aristocratic clergy, and low poor rates', and the villages black with coal dust, noisy with the rattle of handlooms, and broken by Dissent. There was a variety about George Eliot's childhood surroundings that might well cause her to speculate about society.

George Eliot's father married twice, and she was the last of her father's five and of her mother's three children. She was

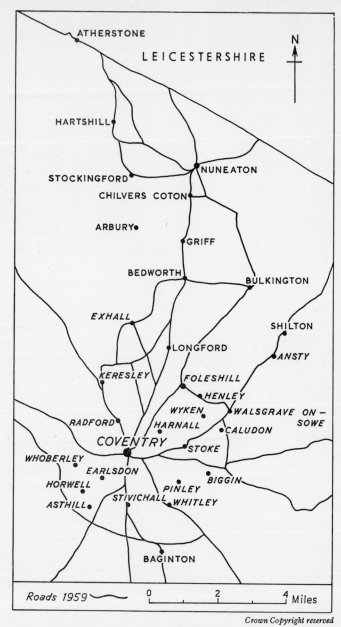

N

ATHERSTONE

LEICESTERSHIRE

HARTSHILL

STOCKINGFORD

NUNEATON

CHILVERS COTON

ARBURY

GRIFF

BEDWORTH

BULKINGTON

EXHALL

SHILTON

LONGFORD

ANSTY

KERESLEY

FOLESHILL

HENLEY

WYKEN

WALSGRAVE ON - SOWE

RADFORD

HARNALL

CALUDON

COVENTRY

STOKE

WHOBERLEY

EARLSDON

BIGGIN

HORWELL

PINLEY

STIVICHALL

WHITLEY

ASTHILL

BAGINTON

Roads 1959   0   2   4 Miles

FIG. 1. Coventry and the weaving area. Places in italics were included in the county of the city of Coventry.

born in 1819, and was christened Mary Ann. She generally wrote her letters to her friends over the name Marian, and in addressing a wider public she chose for her novels the pseudonym, George Eliot. Her grown-up life, and her relations with Chapman, Spencer, and Lewes, attracted as much attention from her contemporaries as her childhood and youth have since attracted from her biographers. A new book about her has been published, on the average, once a year for the last thirty years, and faced with the embarrassing task of choosing between them one can do no better than to turn straight to her letters, which have been published in seven volumes by Gordon S. Haight, and to the novels themselves. Both are extraordinarily revealing.

She was a plain girl with a passionate desire for masculine affection. At first she made an idol of her brother Isaac, as Maggie Tulliver made an idol of Tom in *The Mill on the Floss*; then, when Isaac grew older and was tired of playing with her, she transferred her affections to her father, whose solid virtues are commemorated at length in Adam Bede and more concisely in Caleb Garth in *Middlemarch*. Her mother meant much less to her than her father, for her mother had conferred a favour on Robert Evans by consenting to be his second wife, and did not hesitate to remind him of it. Mary Ann was expected to rise to the standards of her mother's side of the family, and there were Tullivers and Dodsons in her young life, just as there were in Maggie's.

George Eliot was not, therefore, a very well-adjusted child. But being both a clever and a serious one, she soon exhausted the resources of her first teachers, and when she was thirteen she was sent to the Misses Franklin's school at Coventry. Languages and music were added to her accomplishments, but the piety preached and practised there fostered the tendencies to introspection and self-mortification with which this young girl had come out into the world. The Franklins' evangelical morality was altogether too black and too white for somebody who had already begun to wonder whether the world was not, and ought not to be, morally, all shades and many colours,[1] while visiting the poor only served to increase George Eliot's

[1] See, George Eliot, *Scenes of Clerical Life*, 'The Sad Fortunes of the Rev. Amos Barton', Chapter IV.

doubts whether she herself had any right to enjoy life at all.

By this time it was certain that George Eliot could never be luxuriously, carelessly happy, and that if she was to reach the peace of mind of a person who has come to terms with the world, it would have to be by intellectual conviction. Intellectually, she was both incapable of taking things as she found them, and too honest to take refuge in a creed which did not answer all her questions. Emotionally, she needed a man to draw her out, and to help her to make the intellectual advance by which alone her happiness could be achieved. This was her predicament, unformulated, perhaps, in her own mind for all her questioning, at the moment when she left school, and left Coventry, in 1835, to return home to nurse her sick mother. After her mother died, she stayed on to keep house for her father, her doubt remaining unresolved, and her character undeveloped by her work about the house. This was her position for six years until 1841, when her father retired, handed over his business to his son, and came with Mary Ann to live at Bird Grove on the northern outskirts of Coventry.

CHARLES BRAY

It was not long now before George Eliot came under the influence of Charles Bray, who did so much to form her opinions, and who has left so delightful an account of their friendship.[1] Bray was a free-thinker, a phrenologist, and a philosopher, who is said to have proposed to Caroline Hennell on the day they met. With such precipitancy he went through life, embracing new ideas before he fully understood them, and remaining faithful to them all his life.

Bray was born in 1811, eight years before George Eliot: a delicate child, both his schooling and his early career in business in London were interrupted by illness.[2] In his spare time he read widely and seriously. By 1830 he had begun to doubt the truth of Christianity, and his doubt soon hardened into disbelief. In 1835, before he met Caroline, he discovered the 'science' of phrenology. With his phrenological mind's eye he must have measured Caroline before he made his proposal:

[1] Charles Bray, *Phases of Opinion and Experience during a Long Life*, 1884, pp. 72-78.
[2] The details are from Charles Bray, *Phases of Opinion*, &c., 1884, p. 2.

my wife and I were of very different dispositions, she possessing what I most wanted. She was exceedingly reserved, I too open: (Cautiousness and Secretiveness small) 'a leaky fool', as George Eliot calls Mr. Brooke in *Middlemarch*.[1]

The Brays and the Hennells were both Coventry families, ribbon manufacturers' families, and Caroline was a London Hennell, a cousin.

In 1840 the Brays set up house at Rosehill. The house has disappeared, but there is an engraving of it in J. W. Cross's *Letters of George Eliot*. It was

far enough from the town for country quiet, and yet near enough to hear the sweet church bells and the chimes of St. Michael's, with the distant hum of the city, which gave a cheerful sense of the world being alive on weekdays, and the peaceful lull that told that it was enjoying its respite on the Sunday.[2]

There the Brays entertained. In the summer they would spread a bear-skin on the lawn under the acacia, and there their friends would sit and talk. Many people came to see them: Caroline's brother Charles, prompted at her instance to reply to her husband's freethinking with the *Inquiry concerning the Origin of Christianity*, one of the most important sympathetic criticisms of the Bible in the nineteenth century; Dr. Connolly, the reformer of lunatic asylums; George Combe, the great phrenologist, with Mrs. Combe the daughter of Sarah Siddons, who would sometimes fall asleep in the middle of her husband's calm, wise discourse, 'her head inclined towards him in a reverent attitude of attention'; James Simpson, the promoter of national education; George Dawson, a popular preacher; Herbert Spencer, the sociologist; and Emerson, on his visit to England in 1847.[3]

CHARLES BRAY AND GEORGE ELIOT

George Eliot was introduced to this circle by Charles Bray's sister, Mrs. Sibree. Alarmed by her brother's free-thinking, and impressed by the apparent strength of George Eliot's evangelical opinions, Mrs. Sibree thought that in a head-on collision the Lord would look after his own, and that evangelical piety would

[1] ibid, p. 47. The reference to *Middlemarch* is on p. 691 in the World's Classics edition, 1947.

[2] Charles Bray, *Phases of Opinion*, &c., 1884, pp. 69-70.   [3] ibid, pp. 70-71.

triumph. It happened the other way round; George Eliot's evangelicalism evaporated, until the day, so heartbreaking to her father, when she refused to go to Sunday service. George Eliot and her father separated, and although they were later reconciled, the old bond was broken for ever. Robert Evans died in 1849 : George Eliot never rejoined the church.

What Christianity lost by the defection of George Eliot, was not lost to humanity. Here too she followed in the footsteps of Charles Bray. The rejection of the doctrine of the atonement did not relieve one from an obligation to one's neighbour or a duty to oneself, and the need for self-improvement remained as strong as ever. Charles Bray's creed enabled George Eliot to realize herself. Through him she discovered that religion could be cast off without abandoning either reverence or morality. Charles Bray's lesser mind enabled George Eliot's greater one to resume its march to self-fulfilment. How this came about is not explained by either of them. Charles Bray was somebody to lean upon, but there is no suggestion that they were either of them in love. If Charles Bray momentarily satisfied George Eliot's emotional craving, it was by companionship and nothing else. Nor was there anything suggested to her by Bray's intellect that her own could not over-reach. But this does not preclude Bray's having brought to her problems, which had once been his own, an answer that she had not dared to formulate for herself, and friendship of a kind that inspired her to adopt it. It is no wonder that she began to contribute to the reviews with Bray's help, nor that, as her confidence grew and as she progressed beyond Bray, she was carried away from Coventry altogether.

This is not the place to discuss Charles Bray's philosophy at length. His one original idea was that all matter had at one time acted intelligently.

But, just as in our own case, an act which was performed at first with conscious intelligence comes by dint of repetition to be performed automatically, so the conscious intelligence which once pervaded the world has subsided in the ages into automatic action, constituting what we call natural laws.[1]

---

[1] The extract is from an article in the *Westminster Review* for April 1879 which summarizes Bray's philosophy.

See, too, Charles Bray, *The Science of Man*, 1868, p. 224.

Thus the only difference between animate and inanimate matter is one of habit, and the unity of nature may be said to transcend the distinction between the two. The rest of Bray's philosophy was a combination of every contemporary idea. He was an optimist, picking up a bit here and a bit there, and twisting it all together into one long tangled thread of incompatibilities. He tried to retain the advantages of agnosticism while reconciling them with a belief in God: he tried to be a relativist and a transcendentalist at the same time, and to believe both in determinism and self-help.

Briefly, his so-called philosophy of Necessity, or Causation, took it for granted that cause and effect, or rather antecedence and consequence, are all we can ever know, in the mental as in the physical world.[1] Every action has a cause, and given the motives that are present to the individual mind, and given likewise the character and dispositions of the individual, the manner in which he will act may be unerringly inferred.[2] This does away with the scriptural idea of free will, though necessity is not opposed, Bray said, to that which is voluntary, but to that which is contingent.[3] Things could never, therefore, have been other than they are, and regret and remorse are both pointless. But this does not mean that there is no such thing as vice, for if, in accordance with our moral duty, we study the nature of man and of everything around us, we shall find that since certain causes produce certain effects, we can, as Robert Owen believed, mould man as we would have him. We can educate our children (within the limits posed by the bumps on their heads), to be the children we desire.[4] Paradoxically, we can escape from inevitability, even if the paradox leads, as George Eliot suggests, with an apparently innocent, but deadly word of sabotage worthy of Celia, to the conclusion that we should hang the parents of a murderer.[5]

George Eliot did not swallow Bray's philosophy whole. What she did adopt from it, as Bray claims in his autobiography,[6] was

[1] Charles Bray, *The Philosophy of Necessity*, 2nd. edn., 1863, pp. 1, 2.

[2] ibid, p. 26.   [3] ibid, pp. 21-22.

[4] Charles Bray, *The Science of Man*, 1868, pp. 230-1, p. 112, and *The Philosophy of Necessity*, 2nd edn., 1863, p. 7.

[5] George Eliot, *Middlemarch*, World's Classics, 1947, p. 179.

[6] Charles Bray, *Phases of Opinion*, &c., 1884, p. 73.

a belief in the doctrine of consequences, and a very important and rather German belief in the extent to which we are all influenced by each other, the extent to which 'we insignificant people with our daily words and acts are preparing the lives of many Dorotheas'.[1] In all her novels she took care to draw the characters and circumstances of her heroes and heroines clearly enough for the story to work itself out with an agreeable certainty. Her heroes do not triumph over circumstances in complete control of their own actions, like those of her early favourite Sir Walter Scott, nor yet are they sported with by the Fates, like Hardy's. George Eliot's novels achieve what, if we look at Bray's philosophy logically, is a paradox, the reconciliation of determinism and self-help. In this way *Middlemarch* reads like a work of labour while the stage is being set and peopled, and then the story sweeps on, writing itself, for the author's mind and the reader's mind are both clear, and the rest follows as surely as the foundations are well laid.

It is at this point that George Eliot advances beyond Charles Bray. The distinction between determinism and free will is more convincing when it is set out in her analysis, than it is when it is baldly set out in his paradox. Charles Bray draws a line, which he calls the present. On one side of this line is the past, which could not have been different, and on the other is the future, which can be what we choose to make it. George Eliot rejects this rigid distinction, and goes on to measure how far our own and other people's actions in the past are determining our actions now, and how far our own and other people's actions now are going to determine our actions in the future. George Eliot's frontier between free will and determinism is a line drawn through a continuum of past, present, and future, where actions in the present, whether they are determined or whether they are free, cannot help but help to determine actions in the future. This is an altogether subtler and more satisfying conception than Bray's. It fills her novels with what is, in fact, a philosophy of history, and it establishes her in the front rank of nineteenth century sociologists.

Her importance in nineteenth century history is, however, even greater than this. Her explorations along the frontier between free will and determinism having led her to such an

[1] George Eliot, *Middlemarch*, World's Classics, 1947, p. 896.

exact understanding of the extent to which one action was the consequence of another, she naturally came to judge actions by their consequences, which could be ascertained, rather than by their motives, which could not. Here too she owed much to Bray (and both of them to Bentham), but here again she surpassed him. While her intellect earned her a position of distinction among the most distinguished company of her age, and her moral fervour became the envy even of those who most loathed its basis, her name became identified with the attempt to separate the Siamese twins of morality and religion. No less a person than Lord Acton readily admitted that she was as good as a person could be—who was not a Christian.[1]

Like Bray, George Eliot considered Christianity harmful, because it directed men's attention away from the ascertainable consequences of their actions on earth towards the pursuit of forgiveness in heaven. There were far too many Casaubons among the clergy, wounding their wives while they went about doing what they believed to be their Christian duty. Bray, however, having come to the conclusion that Christianity was harmful, could not resist falling into the Christian trap of speculating on the nature of the Creator.[2] The strength of the agnostic lies in saying 'we do not know', and saying it very loudly. George Eliot disdained to assert her beliefs in a matter where knowledge was necessarily unattainable, and retained the thorough agnostic's advantage of being able to criticize everyone who was less timid. Her consistency was here her strength, and the almost complete absence of malice with which she pointed her criticisms was her chief recommendation.

Bray's freethinking and Bray's philosophy both left their mark on George Eliot. Bray's phrenology she did not swallow, and in her novels the 'science' is ridiculed,[3] though Bray asserts that she was at one time interested in it and had a cast taken of her head. It was a large head, and George Combe, on first seeing the cast, took it for a man's.

The temperament nervous lymphatic, that is, active without endurance, and her working hours were never more than from 9 a.m. to 1 p.m. . . . In her brain development the Intellect greatly

[1] Lord Acton, 'George Eliot's Life', *The Nineteenth Century*, March 1885.

[2] e.g., Charles Bray, *The Science of Man*, 1868, p. 253.

[3] e.g., *Felix Holt*, Chapter 5.

predominates. . . . In the Feelings, the Animal and Moral regions are about equal, the moral being quite sufficient to keep the animal in order and in due subservience, but would not be spontaneously active. The Social feelings were very active, particularly the adhesiveness. She was of a most affectionate disposition, always requiring someone to lean upon, preferring what has hitherto been considered the stronger sex to the other and more impressible.[1]

If Combe and Bray could tell all this from George Eliot's cast, they can be forgiven for believing in the 'science' of phrenology, for no one who has read George Eliot's letters and novels can doubt its accuracy.

The gatherings at Rosehill were Coventry's most important intellectual circle, and Bray and George Eliot the ancient city's only known philosophers. But Bray did not rest on the lawn all day, spinning theories. He had inherited a 'large and lucrative' business from his father in 1835,[2] and for twenty-one years he was a ribbon manufacturer,[3] earning that handle to his name in the British Museum catalogue. Too young to have taken part in municipal affairs at the time the new Liberal Town Council was substituted for the old Tory Corporation in the early thirties, Bray nevertheless took a prominent Radical part in local politics throughout the middle of the century. For some months, while George Eliot was living in his house, he was a member of the Town Council, until, as he says, the shopkeepers turned him out for his part in founding the co-operative society.[4] To help him in his politics he bought the local Liberal newspaper, the *Coventry Herald*, in 1846, and ran it for nearly twenty years in opposition to the Tory *Standard*.[5] George Eliot's only known contributions to the *Herald* were literary, but many of Bray's leading articles on politics or industry must have been talked over with, or in front of her at Rosehill, both before and after publication.

George Eliot was familiar with Charles Bray's warehouse in Much Park Street,[6] and it was natural for her to include a ribbon manufacturer, Mr. Vincy, in *Middlemarch*. Middlemarch

[1] Charles Bray, *Phases of Opinion*, &c., 1884, pp. 74-75.

[2] ibid, p. 20.   [3] ibid, p. 89.   [4] ibid, p. 68.

[5] Charles Bray, *Phases of Opinion*, &c., 1884, p. 81.

[6] George Eliot's, *Letters*, edited by Gordon S. Haight, Vol. II, p. 20, 27 April 1852, George Eliot to Mr. and Mrs. Charles Bray.

is Coventry.[1] Realizing that ribbons are not the stuff of which novels are made, she does not, however, say much about Mr. Vincy's trade. The historical value of *Middlemarch* is that, in 1868, George Eliot knew that in writing about the Middlemarch of 1830-32, she was writing about old provincial society. The novel is historically accurate, not in the sense that individual characters can be identified, but in its nice sense of the distinctions between ranks, and of the links that still held the different ranks together in a single society. There is a faithful representation of the line between county and manufacturing families, and of the gulf between the old manufacturers and those in retail trade. The relationship of the country villages to the town is accurately portrayed, with weaving and squalor in the villages on one side of the city, and agriculture and prosperity in the villages on the other. Above all, however, George Eliot, with her philosophy, and with her acute perception of the way in which men have to suffer for each other's sins, was ideally suited to discover and to describe the elusive currents of public opinion which determined the standards of conduct in an old provincial town. *Middlemarch* ends with the disgrace of Mr. Bulstrode, the banker. But Mr. Vincy would have been in disgrace too in 1830, had he tried to overthrow the customs of his trade. By 1868, as George Eliot knew, things were different, and this would no longer have been true.

Charles Bray did not find making ribbons a satisfying intellectual outlet. He wrote an essay on *The Union of Agriculture and Manufactures*, and there are two leading articles in the *Coventry Herald* in 1850,[2] and a passage in the second edition of the *Philosophy of Necessity*, published in 1863, in which he follows up the ideas in the essay.[3] These read like a cross between an advertisement for a Chartist land scheme and a description of the Garden of Eden, but they do form a theoretical basis, however meagre and however idealistic, for the unique development in Coventry of the cottage factory system. Two other essays, one upon the employment of women in industry in Coventry, which was read to the British Association in 1857, and the other upon Councils of Conciliation and Boards of Arbitration,

---

[1] See Appendix below, pp. 143-5.

[2] The *Coventry Herald*, 11 July, and 18 July 1850.

[3] Charles Bray, *The Philosophy of Necessity*, 2nd edn., 1863, p. 410.

written in 1861 after the collapse of the trade and the great strike, promise well. But here one misses the amassed statistics and the sense of social purpose that are found in many of the 'blue books' of the age. With reference to the strike, Bray makes the same exhortation to masters and men to bury the hatchet that is heard after every serious industrial dispute. But there is no examination of the causes of the struggle, and no attempt to explain why, at that particular time, both sides were resolved, whatever the cost, to concede nothing. Bray was intelligent enough to see that the masters did not go bankrupt, and the men go hungry for fun, but his inquiries were not painstaking enough to reveal to him the bitter sense of injustice felt on both sides. His leading articles in the *Herald*, however, are more revealing than he knew, for they show this child of an old manufacturing family, whose father would have thought in terms of the list of prices, talking in the new language of political economy, and of the wages fund.[1] Bray himself is therefore typical of some of the changes that transformed the old society into the new.

But there is much about Coventry, if not about its trades, in Bray's autobiography published in 1884, *Phases of Opinion and Experience during a Long Life*, a charming book, written as the shadows lengthened on a calm and reflective retirement. In it he tells how, as a young man, he gained the whole of this world by ceasing to regard it as a preparation for the next.[2] Enthusiastically he tried to persuade others to follow him: sorrowfully, but without recrimination, he saw them go on their way, unaffected by anything he said. Bray was too philanthropic, and he lacked the powers of concentration needed to make a success of business, and he came down in the world. But it is said of him that he never regretted it, and was always happy[3]—a fortunate result that must be attributed either to his philosophy or to his disposition. In politics he was too restless and too impatient to become a leader, too original and too independent to become a representative. He could not reform the city in a blaze of electoral success. He was sensitive and easily wounded, but a man of this stamp, who does not bear

---

[1] e.g. the *Coventry Herald*, 1 August 1850.

[2] Charles Bray, *Phases of Opinion*, &c., 1884, p. 19.

[3] Verbal communication from Mr. Walter Dunn.

malice, may yet be extremely persuasive in private among his friends, and through his newspaper among the public at large.

JOSEPH GUTTERIDGE

After the ribbon manufacturer comes the ribbon weaver. *Lights and Shadows in the Life of an Artisan*, published in 1893, is the slightly pretentious title to a book that would not have seemed pretentious sixty years ago. Joseph Gutteridge, the author, was a Coventry weaver who never rose beyond the margin of employment and unemployment. His life, nevertheless, as the preface points out, shows how true happiness can be independent of, and rise above, mere material circumstance. This is part of the creed of nineteenth century Liberalism, and Gutteridge reveals all the self-righteousness, indignation, and independence of the nineteenth century English Liberal.

To give an instance of his self-righteousness: he recalls how at one time he was not on speaking terms with his brother on account of 'my remonstrance with him in respect of a young woman with whom he kept company' :[1] so, too, with his son, who had got into bad company, and was 'fast drifting to degradation'.[2] Yet when Joseph Gutteridge himself, not yet out of his apprenticeship, had determined to marry, and his uncles had remonstrated with him, justly, on the improvidence of such a step, he had been upset by their interference, and married in spite of them.[3] Gutteridge had all the delight of his age in pointing out to other people how wrong they were, and how much better they might be. Without wishing to interfere in other people's affairs (which was illiberal), Gutteridge was never afraid to say what he would do in their place.

As an example of his Liberal sense of indignation and independence, there is his refusal, having served his seven years' apprenticeship, to take his freedom, because of the iniquitous stamp duty of £1. 0s. 6d.[4] Why should I, having served my bondage for seven years, have to purchase my freedom?, he asked, and vowed never to take it while the duties lasted.

---

[1] Joseph Gutteridge, *Lights and Shadows in the Life of an Artisan*, 1893, p. 68.

[2] ibid, p. 96.   [3] ibid, pp. 46, 49.

[4] The fees, which were £1. 0s. 6d. for the stamp and parchment, and 3s. to the Town Clerk, were regulated by 21 George III, public, c. liv. See below p. 28.

Either of the two political parties would have paid the duties for him, he adds significantly, for then he would have had a vote.[1] But Gutteridge preferred his independence, and it was seven years before the duties were abolished, and he became a freeman and a voter. Independent he remained: rather than go on the parish when out of work, he starved, and his wife and children starved with him.

For two days not a particle of food . . . passed our lips, and for nearly a fortnight, in . . . bitterly cold weather, we . . . slept on the bare boards huddled together to keep as warm as we could.[2]

Such self-righteousness, such indignation, and such independence were three of the virtues of that Liberal age. They remind one of that greatest of all self-righteous, indignant, and independent Victorians, Mr. Gladstone. No wonder then that a copy of Gutteridge's book should have been sent to him, and that he, struck with sympathy for the author, should have made him a present of one hundred pounds.[3] One can sense the passages Mr. Gladstone must have liked best. There was a real affinity between these two men, separated as they were by half the social classes in the kingdom, and this affinity helps, incidentally, to explain the strength of Liberalism in England. It was the disappearance of the Gutteridges at one end of the scale as much as the disappearance of the Gladstones at the other that killed the Liberal party.

But just as the strength of character of Gladstone and Gutteridge was the strength of the Liberal party, so the want of a connexion between them was its weakness. It would be unfair to say that all Gladstone ever did for the working classes was to give a hundred pounds, privately, to one individual. But Bray, who never knew of this gift, had already put his finger on the weakness of the Liberal party's position. The political economy of the present day wants a moral region, he said in his autobiography, still sticking to the terminology of phrenology,

it is based on unlimited competition, or the ennobling doctrine of 'everyone for himself and devil take the hindmost', and Gladstone is its most powerful and popular representative. With his forty horse

[1] Joseph Gutteridge, *Lights and Shadows*, &c., 1893, p. 58.

[2] ibid, pp. 65, 66.

[3] Verbal communication from Mr. Walter Dunn. There is a copy of Gutteridge's book in the Library at Hawarden.

PLATE I.

b. Joseph Gutteridge.

a. Charles Bray.

talking power he has been able to do much good . . . but whether he has not lowered the tone of Liberalism . . . it will be for history to determine.[1]

The link between Liberalism and *Laisser Faire* was vital; even Bray could not escape the 'logic' of the wages fund, and Liberalism could not outlive the independent working man whose proudest boast was that he had never received a penny in charity.

Gutteridge had, indeed, more pride than he had the means to support. He was born in 1816, the first of three brothers, and his mother died when he was still young. After attending dame and charity schools, he practised his reading by spelling out the names over the shops as he walked past on his way to work. He was apprenticed to his father in Mrs. Dresser's factory in St. Agnes' Lane. But before he was out of his apprenticeship his father died, and Joseph married without waiting to save the money to buy a loom.[2] This was a critical moment in a weaver's career, and Gutteridge felt the effects of his imprudence for the rest of his life, time and again regretting that he was out of work because he had no loom of his own.[3]

But he survived all his troubles, and was chosen to represent the Coventry weavers at the Paris exhibition of 1867.[4] With his ambition to work at home,[5] his combination of Liberal feelings with an intensely conservative attitude towards his trade, and his scepticism towards religion,[6] Joseph Gutteridge was representative of the better class of Coventry weavers. On the other hand his lack of devotion to the list of prices and to the combinations of workmen to enforce it, separated Gutteridge from his fellows. He was a Liberal, not a Labour, working man.

Both Bray and Gutteridge had interests outside their trade. After they had met at the winter lectures of the Coventry Mutual Improvement Society in the fifties, Gutteridge pithily summed up Bray's philosophy as the doctrine of 'when-you-are-dead-you-are-done-with'.[7] Gutteridge's own interests were in

[1] Charles Bray, *Phases of Opinion*, &c., 1884, pp. 28-29.

[2] See Joseph Gutteridge, *Lights and Shadows*, &c., 1893, Chapters I, II, III.

[3] e.g., ibid, p. 60. In regretting that he had no loom of his own Gutterridge was thinking in terms of the old industrial system. As the new factory system spread the outdoor weavers began to find their looms a liability. See below pp. 68, 134.

[4] Joseph Gutteridge, *Lights and Shadows*, &c., 1893, p. 179.

[5] e.g. ibid, p. 64.   [6] ibid, p. 79.   [7] ibid, p. 113.

botany and fossils. He had always loved flowers, roaming the fields outside the city as a child to find them, and writing with enthusiasm as an old man of the gorse and bracken on Hearsall Common in his youth, of the broom, harebell, erica, wood betony, and the pale yellow, cruciform flower of the tormentel.[1] As a boy he scarcely knew their English names: as an old man he could name any wild flower in English and in Latin. But his fossils were his greatest love, and without going far from Coventry, he built up a collection locally famous and nationally known, which overflowed from one room to another of his weaver's house (18 Yardley Street), where everything was neatly arranged in glass cases and clearly labelled. In this house Joseph Gutteridge enjoyed a well earned and respected retirement, passing the time in showing visitors round his 'museum'.[2]

WILLIAM ANDREWS

At least as remarkable in its way as the published life of Joseph Gutteridge is the unpublished diary of William Andrews,[3] who was at once a more single-minded and a more successful man than Gutteridge. Andrews was born in 1835, and accomplished the feat of rising from apprentice designer to ribbon manufacturer in the middle of the sixties, when only the most efficient could survive, let alone prosper. But then Andrews was of the most efficient. There was no false modesty about him —or, at any rate, there is none in his diary. He does not hesitate to tell us that he was the best apprentice and the best designer in the Coventry of his day. What makes him so irritating to the reader is the conviction that he may have been right.

His diary is delightfully frank, and with rare virtue he only confided in it when he had something to say. This is no tedious catalogue of the English climate, but the story of a man who won prizes as an apprentice to go to the Great Exhibition in 1851, and to Paris in 1855. After his apprenticeship he went to Cash's, a firm which still exists, and is known today for the manufacture of name tapes. The brothers Cash play an important part in this story because they built cottage factories at Kingfield in 1856-57, and Andrews plays an important part in

---

[1] Joseph Gutteridge, *Lights and Shadows*, &c., 1893, pp. 8-9.
[2] ibid, p. 164.   [3] This has been placed in the City Record Office.

this story because he was their first manager there. His relations with the brothers Cash are described in detail, from his side. They disagreed in the end—anyone would have disagreed with Andrews in the end—and Andrews worked for several other firms before he saved the small amount of capital needed to set up on his own. Finally, on several occasions in the 1870's, this successful manufacturer acted as the spokesman for the whole trade, and in 1878 he published a little volume of *Papers relating to the Ribbon Trade.*

By the 1860's anyone with a hundred or two hundred pounds could borrow the rest of the money needed to set up in business as a master. Forty or fifty years earlier this would have been impossible, for in the old days the manufacturers traded on their own and not the silk merchant's and the dyer's money.[1] Andrews is typical of a new race of masters—men of small means and sharp talents who helped to transform the ribbon trade in this period. Andrews himself was greatly helped by his remaining a bachelor, in which he was, of course, exceptional. Gutteridge had married before he was out of his apprenticeship, and lived on the margin of employment and prosperity ever after. Andrews, on the other hand, was able, when he was out of work, to have a week's holiday in the south of England.

*　　　*　　　*

Finally, it is worth noticing how closely connected these four Coventrians were. George Eliot lived in Charles Bray's house; Gutteridge met Bray at evening lectures: Andrews worked for the brothers Cash, and the brothers Cash, in their turn, were influenced by Bray to build a cottage factory. When Bray retired from the trade in 1857 they bought his house.[2] It was a closely knit world, though more closely knit in 1830 than in 1860, and this is important because it took a closely knit society to provide the public opinion which supported the list of prices governing the ribbon trade. As society became divided, the list could no longer be maintained. The lives and changing opinions

[1] In the early nineteenth century the opportunity for the employment of small capital in the ribbon trade was limited to the class of men called 'undertakers' (see below pp. 49-50). Several of the charities of the city loaned money to freemen to enable them to set up in business as undertakers, see *Reports Commissioners, 1835,* XXV, p. 393.

[2] Charles Bray, *Phases of Opinion,* &c., pp. 159-60.

of people unconnected with the ribbon trade, as well as the lives and changing opinions of those within the trade itself, were to bring about the transformation. There could be no better vindication of Charles Bray's and George Eliot's doctrine of consequences.

II

THE CITY AND ITS POLITICS

GENERAL DESCRIPTION OF THE CITY

COVENTRY lay naturally at the centre of the roads of medieval England. Its importance was recognized by King Henry VI, who raised the city and the neighbouring villages on the north and east to the status of a county in 1451.[1] These villages had mostly belonged to the countess Godiva in the eleventh century, and for many centuries they and the city together formed a natural, and largely self-sufficient economic unit. Politically, however, the inhabitants of the villages within the county but beyond the city boundary were at a disadvantage. They were barred from the corporate privileges of the city, and in parliamentary elections they were disfranchised, being unable to vote either in the city, where the franchise was confined to the freemen,[2] or for the northern division of the county of Warwickshire.

So long as English industry was based upon wool, Coventry had a fair claim to be the commercial and industrial centre of the Midlands. But in the new age of coal and iron Coventry, which had coal but no iron, gradually gave way to Birmingham and the Black Country, which had both, and some time before the beginning of the nineteenth century Coventry had ceased to be a great provincial capital. But in 1830 the main road from London to Holyhead and Ireland still passed through the city, and the people of Coventry remained in touch with the news passing along this great highway. In 1828 Telford re-made the road, and straightened its course both into and out of Coventry. As the traffic increased, more and more coaches stopped to

---

[1] Radford, Keresley, Foleshill, Exhall, Ansty, Caludon, Wyken, Henley-le-Wood-End, Stoke, Biggin, Whitley, Pinley, Harnall, and part of Sowe. These all lay to the north or east of the city. In addition, the county included Whoberley to the west, Asthill and Horwell to the south-west, and part of Stivichall to the south (see figure 1, p. 2).

[2] See below, p. 28.

change horses at the inns of the city, while the passengers got
out to take refreshment.

But the local gentry, who felt that they had been encouraged
by the government to invest their savings in the various trusts
for the improvement of the road,[1] had not been adequately
rewarded from the tolls when the London to Birmingham
railway was opened in the autumn of 1838. Their complaints,
and the lamentations of the innkeepers, went unheeded as the
railway drained the traffic off the road. Far from dispelling
the sense of provincial inferiority that George Eliot attributes to
the people of Middlemarch in the period 1830-32,[2] the railway
must have made them more conscious than ever of their own
unimportance. The express coaches had stopped: the express
trains only whistled as they rushed on to Birmingham or
London, and in 1841 the *Coventry Herald*, exaggerating no doubt,
complained that goods intended for London had often to be
taken all the way to Birmingham to be put on the train, while
goods sent down to Coventry from London were frequently
'whirled by their own doors and carried down to Birmingham',
where the owners had to meet them with a cart.[3]

The truth was that Coventry had very little use for the railway. If Coventry wanted coal, barges brought it down the canal
from the collieries at Newgate and Griff, as they had done
since 1769. Coventry's staple manufactures, silk ribbons and
watches, were light, as was becoming in an inland town, and
they were easily transported by coach. The ribbons were packed
in baskets, boxes, and leather bags. Small parcels and goods
wanted quickly went by the fast coaches, at a cost of $1\frac{1}{2}d$. per
lb. Goods sent by van cost $1d$. per lb., while, in both cases, there
was an additional charge for booking.[4] The railway was
cheaper, parcels over 30 lb. being charged at the rate of 5s. per
cwt. in the middle forties, and at as low a rate as 2s. 6d. per cwt.
in the fifties.[5] But the volume of goods entering and leaving
Coventry was probably not sufficient for cheap freight to

---

[1] *The Probable Effects of the Proposed Railway from Birmingham to London considered*,
1831.

[2] George Eliot, *Middlemarch*, World's Classics, 1947, pp. 153, 167, 184, 372, 646,
705, &c.

[3] The *Coventry Herald*, 17 September 1841.   [4] Odell's Diary, City Record Office.

[5] The figures are taken from weekly advertisements in the *Coventry Herald*, and the
Coventry Standard.

compensate the city for the declining traffic on the Holyhead road.

The first thing that must have struck the visitor to Coventry in 1830 was that it was a small, dirty, densely built town, surrounded by pastures and park (see figure 2). The city was three-quarters surrounded by land that could not be built on until it had been enclosed by Act of Parliament. The Act was not forthcoming, and no matter how much the population increased, all the way round the compass from the south-east, through the south and the west, to the north, the people of Coventry were hemmed in by open spaces. The principal factor in constricting the town was the Lammas and Michaelmas land, over which the freemen of the city exercised a right of pasture. Linked with this land were various commons, and Cheylesmore Park, formerly part of the lands of the Duchy of Cornwall, which had been leased to the Marquis of Hertford in 1789, and on the expiry of the lease thirty years later, sold to him outright.[1]

The Lammas and Michaelmas lands covered about 1,000 acres, and were therefore much more important than the commons, which only covered 300. For half the year they were enclosed, and belonged exclusively to their proprietors, but from Lammas (1 August) till Candlemas (2 February) in the case of Lammas lands, and from Michaelmas (29 September) till Candlemas (2 February) in the case of Michaelmas lands, the freeman had a right of pasture over them for two horses and one cow, or two cows and one horse, and the fences had to be broken down so that the animals might graze freely.[2] This custom, sensible enough in the fourteenth century, when the citizens found it hard to feed their animals in the winter, was widely recognized by the middle of the nineteenth century to have put a stop to the development of the city, by making it literally hidebound. This was one reason why Birmingham had grown, and not Coventry. The land was good, but the proprietors could not exploit it properly because it had to be kept as pasture, and

---

[1] B. Poole, *Coventry, Its History and Antiquities*, 1869, p. 18.

[2] There are accounts of the Lands in the *Coventry Standard*, 19 September 1856; *Reports Commissioners, 1835*, XXV, pp. 393, 400, 431; William Ranger, *Report to the General Board of Health on a preliminary inquiry into the Sewerage, Drainage, and Supply of Water, and the Sanitary Condition of the Inhabitants of the City of Coventry*, 1849, pp. 7-9; and Mary Dormer Harris, *The Story of Coventry*, 1911, Chapter XII.

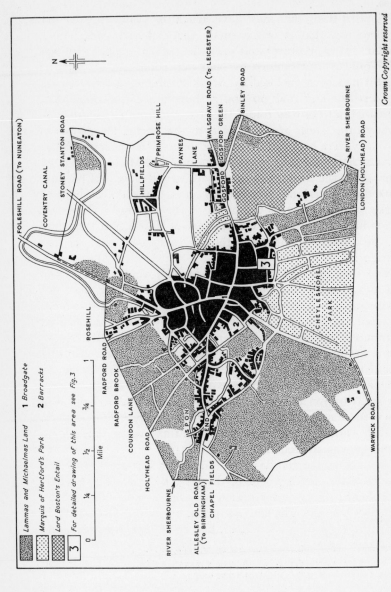

FIG. 2. Coventry, showing the area remaining to the city after the boundary changes following the reform of the municipal corporations in 1835.

every year the fences had to be alternately pulled down and repaired. Nor did the freemen find their right very valuable, for the proprietors naturally did their best to exhaust the pasture before throwing it open. It is not surprising that only a small number of the freemen exercised their rights.[1] This minority of the freemen, in a town where the freemen were themselves a minority of the population, was nevertheless to prove strong enough, thanks to the peculiar organization of politics in the town, to prevent all attempts for many years to enclose the lands and extinguish the rights of pasture.

Add the Lammas and Michaelmas lands, the commons, and the Park together, and except for Hillfields, there is only one large gap left round the city. That is to the south of Gosford, between Gosford and Stoke on the one side, and the river Sherbourne on the other. This land too was not available for building, under the terms of the entail by which it had come to Lord Boston.[2] It was not disentailed until 29 September 1860, in the Court of Chancery, and was to be developed in a later period. There remain only one or two small pieces of land round the city not accounted for by pasture rights or entails, and these mostly belonged to the many charities of the city. Chapelfields, for instance, the future watchmakers' area, which was used in the 1830's as a nursery garden,[3] belonged to Sir Thomas White's charity, and the land could not be sold and developed without an Act of Parliament which was not obtained until 1845.[4]

Only in one quarter, in 1830, in Hillfields to the north-east of the city, and in the east between Hillfields and Gosford, was land being developed. Even Hillfields, however, could not be fully joined to Coventry while the river Sherbourne, which divided the city from this new town, was obstructed by two old mills which caused it to flood. These mills too could not be pulled down without an Act of Parliament, not obtained by the City Council until 1844.[5] On every side, then, in the 1830's, Coventry was enclosed by a grip that could be broken only by

[1] The report of the Commissioner appointed to inquire into the Municipal Corporations says 'not above a fourth', *Reports Commissioners, 1835*, XXV, p. 431. William Ranger says 300-500, *Report to the General Board of Health*, &c., 1849, p. 8. Charles Bray says 300, *Phases of Opinion*, &c., 1884, pp. 82-83.

[2] Irby Deeds, Coventry Corporation Deeds.

[3] B. Poole, *Coventry, Its History and Antiquities*, 1869, p. 397.

[4] 8 and 9 Vict., private, c. xvii.   [5] 7 and 8 Vict., local and personal, c. lxxvi.

Act of Parliament. Local Acts being often difficult, and sometimes expensive to obtain, the city had for a long time accepted
the fact that it was unable to expand, and grown up within
itself. While the pressure grew, and the population increased
from 16,034 in 1801 to 30,781 in 1841, small pieces of the
Lammas and Michaelmas lands had been enclosed, first for the
improvement of the Holyhead road, and then for the construction of the railway, and these small enclosures stimulated some
of the citizens to press for the extinction of the Lammas and
Michaelmas lands altogether.[1] The order in which the parts of
the encircling ring were broken determined the course of the
city's expansion over the next seventy years.

Until the freemen could agree to the extinction of their rights
of pasture, both they and the rest of the people of Coventry had
to live in a very congested city. In 1830 most of the inhabitants
still lived and worked at home, and only on the south, round
Warwick Row, was there a purely residential area. In the centre
of the city, shops, warehouses, slaughter-houses, and ribbon
manufactories were crowded together, almost up to the walls of
St. Michael's and Holy Trinity churches, whose two lovely
spires dominated the city. The land had been built on
indiscriminately, and the only appearance of order was
presented by the dyers, whose factories were concentrated along
the upper reaches of the river Sherbourne, where it came into
the city, unpolluted by sewage, at Spon End.[2] The watch
manufacturers too were tending to concentrate their warehouses in the west of the city, along Spon Street, but the
workmen they employed were still scattered all over the ten
wards of the old city.[3] The other trades had to fit in as best they
could, the brewers apparently taking their water from the
Sherbourne after the dyers had finished with it.

In 1831 Coventry contained 5,887 inhabited houses. In
proportion the streets were few, and though by the standards of
the time they were not especially narrow, they were often
congested by the open-air markets. The centre of the city's life

[1] B. Poole, *Coventry, Its History and Antiquities*, 1869, pp. 313-14, and Charles
Bray, *Phases of Opinion*, &c., 1884, p. 83.

[2] Ordnance Survey of 1851.

[3] Verbal communication from Miss Joan Lancaster, who is studying the Census
Records for the City.

was Broadgate, where the crowds gathered during Parliamentary elections, and upon which both the annual Godiva procession in June, and the occasional processions of unemployed weavers converged. The pride of the city in the 1830's must have been Hertford Street, newly laid out under the authority of an Act of Parliament of 1812,[1] and already tending to become the centre of business because it was the centre of banking. The best known and most populous thoroughfare was the spine of the city, part of a main road from Leicester through Coventry to Birmingham, which wound through the city for one and a half miles from Gosford Green in the east, to Spon End in the west. The first half of this road from Gosford Green to Broadgate was called successively Far Gosford Street, Gosford Street, Jordan Well, Earl Street, and High Street, and the second half from Broadgate to Spon End was called Smithford Street, Fleet Street, and Spon Street. The Holyhead road, whose general direction was from south-east to north-west, did not avoid Coventry altogether, as the engineers had wanted it to,[2] but, as a concession to the Coventry shopkeepers, joined this spine road at the end of Jordan Well, and left it at the beginning of Spon Street, so that the passengers from London to Ireland had to traverse a large part of Coventry on their way. To say that the spine of the city was one and a half miles long, is, however, to give a misleading impression of the size of the whole city, which, from north to south, was nowhere more than one thousand yards across, while in Far Gosford Street it only extended as far as the houses on either side of the road. Even in 1860 the city was still small enough for one man with a hand-bell to walk the round of the wards to summon the weavers to a union meeting.[3]

Built up to the ancient streets of the city were many fine, half-timbered houses, which had been erected by the prosperous cloth merchants of the sixteenth and seventeenth centuries. Among them were many plainer but still handsome brick houses of the early eighteenth century. At the time they were built many of these houses had looked out onto extensive gardens laid out at the back, where the citizens had grown their own vegetables and fruit. As the population began to increase

---

[1] 52 George III, local and personal, c. lvii.

[2] T. W. Whitley, *Coventry Coaching and Coach Roads*, reprinted from the *Coventry Herald*, October 1887.

[3] The *Coventry Standard*, 13 July 1860.

about the middle of the eighteenth century and land became more valuable, many of these houses were bought by speculators, who in accordance with the standards of the time, built rows of little cottages down both sides of the gardens if they were wide enough, and down one side if they were not. The dwellings and the courts thus erected behind the older houses were soon occupied, while some of the speculators probably retired to live outside the city on their rents. Faced with an expanding population and with no new land to build on, Coventry was thus, like other cities of which Nottingham is the classic example, solving its problem unhealthily by building in on itself. As one garden after another was built over in this way, the original houses as often as not continued to face the street, while behind them, through the entries, lived a majority of the ordinary people of Coventry. At the same time market gardens sprang up outside the city to supply the growing population with vegetables and fruit, while the surrounding countryside enjoyed an expanding market for its dairy products.

The full extent of this process of in-growth is shown on the map, (figure 3), copied from the Ordnance Survey of 1851. The number of people living in the area shown, which is about 200 yards long and 120 yards wide, can be estimated at about 1,000. Whole areas of the city were like this, and in these crowded courts and yards the people lived with too little air, bad water taken from a standpipe, or possibly a well, which served a dozen or several dozen families, and with cesspits and no main sewer. There was no paving and lighting in the courts, though many of the streets were paved and lighted after a fashion by the Street Commissioners established by an Act of Parliament of 1790.[1] It was no part of the standard of living of the ordinary Coventry family to have direct access to a road, for they never possessed anything which could not be carried down an entry from the shop round the corner—and back again to the pawnbroker's in time of trouble.

THE FREEMEN AND THE PARLIAMENTARY POLITICS OF THE CITY

The freemen who held the key to this state of affairs were themselves almost as much a survival of medieval society as the

[1] 30 George III, public, c. lxxvii.

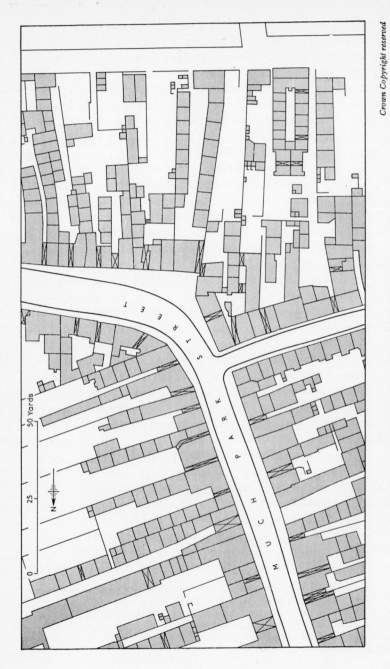

FIG. 3. The old city: detail, showing individual houses.

Lammas lands. Coventry had retained to an extent unequalled
by other cities the custom of freedom by servitude. Every boy or
girl could gain the freedom of the city by serving a registered
apprenticeship to one trade for seven years. The apprentice
could change masters, and many had to because their masters
failed or died, but he must not change trades. Any trade would
do, and while weavers and watchmakers predominated, there
were also apprentice hairdressers, grocers, chimney-sweeps, and
plumber-painter-glaziers. Many of the city's charities encouraged children to become apprentices.[1] The freedom thus
won by servitude brought with it the parliamentary franchise,
and it may have been because the franchise could be exercised
only by men, that very few parents made their daughters serve
the full period. Having finished his seven long years, the
apprentice had still, as Gutteridge found, to pay £1. 3s. 6d.
before his name could be put upon the electoral roll.[2]

The most significant thing about this parliamentary franchise
was that before the 1832 Reform Act the seven years'
apprenticeship was the only qualification for voting for the two
Members who represented the city in the House of Commons.
The Coventry Election Act of 1781, following a resolution of the
House of Commons in 1722, declared that the freemen by
servitude were the only people in Coventry allowed to vote.[3]
No matter how wealthy, no matter how respectable, no matter
how influential you were, unless you had completed a seven
years' apprenticeship to one trade you could not have the
parliamentary vote. The freeman himself, of course, lost the
vote for twelve months if he accepted poor relief from the parish.

All this naturally gave a character of their own to the
Coventry elections.[4] The electorate was large, and in 1790,
when the population can hardly have been more than 14,000,
no fewer than 2,524 freemen were polled.[5] Furthermore, the
electorate was a working class or popular one, made up, not of
the mob, though there was a mob in Coventry, but of the
respectable artisans. At the beginning of the nineteenth century

[1] See the Register of Apprentices' Indentures in the City Record Office.
[2] See above, p. 13, note 4.   [3] 21 George III, public, c. liv.
[4] For the details of the elections at Coventry see T. W. Whitley, *The Parliamentary
Representation of the City of Coventry*, 1894.
[5] On this and other occasions a number of freemen whose work had taken them
to London came back to vote.

the Corporation was accustomed to promote its own candidates at parliamentary elections, and to further their chances by admitting new freemen just before the elections took place, bribing others, and serving gin to the crowds round the polling booth. The freemen sometimes returned Corporation candidates, but they never surrendered the city's independence either to the Corporation or to the county aristocracy, and after the Reform Act of 1832 elections were fought on party lines, and the freemen, with their radical opinions and conservative prejudices, dominated Coventry for thirty years and made it different from other towns.

These were the freemen who held the rights of pasture over the lands that encircled the town. They did not all use their rights, but enough of them did. It would take an Act of Parliament to enclose the Lammas and Michaelmas Lands. The Members for Coventry would have to speak to the Bill for enclosure, and no Member of Parliament for Coventry was going to anticipate the wishes of the freemen in this matter when he depended upon their favour for his re-election. In the 1830's and 1840's every Member for Coventry must have known that both the sitting Members had been turned out in 1826 for failing to attend to their constituents' wishes. So far as the Members of Parliament were concerned, the enclosure of the Lammas lands was politically untouchable until the freemen could agree among themselves to propose it.

This situation was not materially altered by the Reform Act of 1832. The Whigs would have done away with the freemen's vote and established a uniform franchise, but they were thwarted by the House of Lords, and the freemen and the new £10 householders took their places side by side on the new electoral roll. On the new register of electors there were 2,756 freemen, and only 529 of the £10 householders, which meant that the freemen were still in absolute, undivided control of the two seats. By 1840 the freemen had increased to 3,200, and the £10 householders to 589, while for 1850 the figures were 3,506 and 717 respectively. Not until the second Reform Act of 1867 and the introduction of the lodger franchise was the dominance of the freemen brought to an end. In 1867 the city lost one of its two seats, and to elect the single representative there were in 1868, 3,887 freemen and 4,041 other electors.

From 1832 to 1867 the freemen regularly returned Liberal

and Radical Members to the House of Commons, except in 1847 when the Tories won one seat. The majority (of the lowest placed Liberal candidate over the highest placed Tory one) ranged from 35 in 1835 to 1,681 in 1857, and at the seven contested General Elections between 1832 and 1859 it averaged 411. Coventry's most distinguished representative was Edward Ellice, who was elected for the first time in 1818, turned out in 1826, and brought back again in 1830 to represent the city continuously until his death in 1863. Ellice was nicknamed 'the Bear', on account of his extensive business interests in the Hudson's Bay and other North American companies. He was well fitted to represent such a popular electorate, because, as a young man, he had been friendly with radicals like Sir Francis Burdett and Samuel Whitbread. Although he became an under-Secretary in 1832 and Minister at War in 1834, he disliked office, and always preferred independence to responsibility. He looked after his constituents fairly, never canvassing, but always taking the trouble to address public meetings when called upon to explain his conduct in the House. In 1832 his intercession with Lord Melbourne, the Secretary of State, is said to have saved Thomas Burbury and Benjamin Spark from the gallows, after they had been sentenced to death at the Assizes in March for their part in burning down Mr. Beck's factory in 1831.[1] Ellice is also said repeatedly to have refused a peerage, and generally to have shown a lack of side that must have endeared him to the ordinary Coventry weaver.[2]

One can account for the devotion of the freemen to Ellice, but it is not at first sight so easy to account for their devotion to his party. The Whigs and Liberals did not favour the freemen's franchise, and they had tried to abolish it in 1832. The freemen owed their votes to the Tory House of Lords, but they did not as a rule vote Tory. It was the same with free trade. The Whigs and Liberals were the advocates of free trade at a time when Coventry's two trades were both protected, and the Tories were, in theory at least, the advocates of protection. In spite of

[1] See below, p. 48.

[2] The details are from the *Dictionary of National Biography*. The other distinguished men to represent Coventry during this period were Bulwer, the novelist, in 1832, and Sir Joseph Paxton, the architect of the Coventry cemetery (1844) and of the Crystal Palace (1851), who was returned unopposed at a by-election in 1854, and re-elected in 1857 and 1859.

this the ordinary Coventry weaver and the ordinary Coventry watchmaker continued to support the Liberals rather than the Tories, and one must ask why they consistently voted against their own interests.

The answer is primarily psychological. The price of Tory support was subordination. The Tory *Standard* supported the freemen because they were a privileged class. In return the freemen were expected to support the privileges of the governing classes, and in particular of the landlords, who also enjoyed protection. The *Standard* was wrong: the freemen did not cling to the vote because it turned them into a privileged class, but because they had worked for it, and because they wanted to be able to make themselves heard at Westminster.[1] They were not prepared to preserve their own privileges as part of a bargain for preserving other people's on the basis of the Tory assumption that since we are all unequal, all inherited inequalities are good. Finally, if the price of Tory support included Corn Laws for the landlord, the weaver saw no reason why his bread should be kept dear for the benefit of the Earl of Craven at Combe Abbey, or Lord Leigh at Stoneleigh.

The freemen had several answers to the argument that the Coventry trades needed protection, and that they needed a Tory government to preserve it. The freemen generally believed in free trade, on the ground that it would reduce prices in the shops, and their sense of fair play was too strong to allow them to claim protection for the Coventry trades after others had learnt to do without it. They knew that their standard of living was higher than that of their competitors in France and Switzerland, but they believed that their machinery was better, and that the danger to their trades came from 'free labour' rather than from free trade. As for the claim that a Tory government was needed to protect protection, the facts spoke for themselves. It was a Tory government which had removed the prohibition on foreign manufactured silk goods in 1826, and it was Sir Robert Peel himself who reduced the duties again in 1846. Even if protection had been desirable, there was no more to be gained from a Tory government than from a Whig one.

---

[1] In 1837 the Chartist candidate at Coventry polled only 43 votes, but many of the freemen believed, none the less, in the extension of the suffrage, and trusted to the Liberals to achieve it.

THE MUNICIPAL POLITICS OF THE CITY

The freemen never had so much control over the affairs of the city. Officially the government of the town was vested in the Corporation, consisting of the Mayor, ten Aldermen, a Grand Council, and a Second or Common Council. The Common Council had not met for over two hundred years. There were never more than thirty-one people in the Grand Council at one time, and the officers of the Corporation were always members. The Grand Council met annually to elect the officers of the Corporation at the Leet, and the upshot was that for half a century or more before the reform of the municipal corporations in 1835 the government of the city had fallen into the hands of 'a close and self-elected body', in whose appointment the rest of the community had no voice. The whole organization revolved round the Town Clerk, who, in the early 1830's, was a solicitor named Carter. Carter received some perquisites and no salary, but he acted for the Corporation when it went to law, and he remained in private practice in the city. The fees which he could earn in his profession were thus greatly enhanced by his office. Some of the junior offices were irksome, like that of the Chamberlains, who had to collect fees from the freemen for pasturing their animals on the Lammas and Michaelmas lands. These irksome appointments, however, were eagerly sought after, because they were well known to lead to higher office and greater rewards. Among the oligarchs themselves there was a regular *cursus honorum*.[1]

The structure of power was by modern standards corrupt. The Corporation consisted of 'substantial' men, who tried to justify themselves to the rest of the community on the ground that because they were rich they did not need to be paid out of the rates for their work. The rest of the community remained sceptical of their amateur status, and of their disinterestedness, knowing full well that much of the work that was done by amateurs—in paving and lighting the streets for instance—was badly done, and that many of the members of the Corporation could, like the Town Clerk, afford to forego a salary in return for the influence which went with their office. The Corporation had a considerable amount of property, ample rents, and

---

[1] The details are from *Reports Commissioners, 1835*, XXV, pp. 389-91, 424.

revenues from the markets and the fairs. More than £2,000
passed through its hands every year, and, as no accounts were
published, the wildest rumours circulated in the town about the
division of the spoils.[1]

There is no need to believe that the officers of the Corporation
paid money directly into their own pockets. The Corporation
revenues were, nevertheless, often put to a corrupt use, because
the thirty-one members of the oligarchy had to buy support in
the town. This they could do by patronage, and by a judicious
distribution of the wealthy charities of the city, which had
fallen into their hands. Tradesmen could be bought with well
placed contracts for the supply of food and wines for the
Corporation dinners, or for the individual members of the
Corporation themselves. Contracts for sweeping the streets, and
rebuilding the house of correction could be placed, instead of
being put up to tender and sold to the lowest bidder. The
wealthy people of Middlemarch, liked to know when they
bought their tea that they were supporting a tradesman of the
right 'colour'.[2]

The old Corporation enjoyed magisterial powers. The Mayor
was *ex officio* the chairman of the bench, and he was at this time
accustomed to act. The Magistrates had to exercise much
common, political, sense in keeping the peace, for they had only
two weapons, one of them too weak, and the other too strong—
the police, and the military. The constables were between sixty
and eighty in number. There seems to have been competition
for the appointments, which were quite well paid, and the
appointment of the constables provided yet another prop in the
structure of influence by which the old Corporation maintained
itself in power.[3] These constables could catch the individual
thief, but they were powerless, at elections and at the meetings
of unemployed weavers, to control a riot. Until the police were
reorganized in 1834, the Magistrates had often to address
crowds several thousands strong in person, to sympathize with
them, and to persuade them to go home peacefully, or call in
the military from the barracks behind Smithford Street and run

[1] ibid, p. 399. The figure of £2,000 is for the general revenue. In addition the
Corporation controlled many wealthy charities, &c., ibid, p. 404.

[2] George Eliot, *Middlemarch*, World's Classics, 1947, p. 536.

[3] The constables received 2s. 6d. a day, and were never likely to be discharged.
Reports Commissioners, 1835, XXV, p. 393.

the risk of another Peterloo. In these circumstances there was a direct link between popular feeling and the government of the town, and the old Corporation was much more amenable to the wishes of the artisans than its oligarchical constitution would suggest. It was still normal in 1830 for the Magistrates to take the part of the weavers against their masters when they were being paid low wages. Provided the weavers kept the peace, or went no further than a little horseplay, their demonstrations were received with sympathy. If, on the other hand, they resorted to violence, and destroyed property, they lost the support of both the Magistrates and the town.[1]

However satisfactory the old Corporation may, in fact, have been to the ordinary working men of Coventry, nothing could convince them that it was right for it to be based upon privilege and corruption. They tended, therefore, to support the reforming party led by Thomas Banbury and William Browett, which became more vociferous when the central government at last prepared, in July 1833, to follow parliamentary reform with the reform of the municipalities. The two Commissioners sent down from London to investigate the affairs of the city found that there was much to be said against the old Corporation both by way of innuendo and by way of evidence. In their report they criticized its unrepresentative character, its control of the charities, and its handling of accounts.[2]

The main scheme of reform, which was laid down in London, was to be the same for Coventry as for other cities. Only the details were adapted to suit local circumstances. The city was to be divided into six wards, and thirty-six Councillors were to be elected by the burgesses, who were defined as all ratepayers of three years' standing. As a concession to the old selective principle, the thirty-six Councillors were themselves to choose twelve Aldermen and the Mayor. The new City Council was to meet in public, and to publish its accounts. The freemen, who still controlled the parliamentary elections for the city after the Reform Act of 1832, had very little more say in the affairs of the town after the Municipal Corporations Reform Act of 1835 than they had had before it. It is one thing to keep off the parish, and quite another to pay rates, and many of the freemen who contrived to keep out of the arms of the Poor Law and to

---

[1] See below pp. 59-60.   [2] *Reports Commissioners, 1835,* XXV.

retain the parliamentary franchise, were not prosperous enough to pay the local rates and to earn the title of burgess. A small-scale inquiry made in 1838 revealed that out of 161 freemen only 35 were on the burgess list,[1] and in 1840 when there were 3,200 freemen in all, and 3,789 names on the parliamentary electoral roll, there were only 2,173 burgesses.[2]

A new spirit came over the government of the town when the first elections were held at the end of 1835. The Reforming party won 32 out of the 36 seats, and only George Eld and three other Tories survived to represent the old Corporation on the new City Council.[3] The Tories fought hard at the annual elections each November for a number of years after the reform, but they never recovered more than a few seats, and in the 1840's and 1850's many Liberal and Radical candidates were returned unopposed. The new City Council stood primarily, so its supporters said, for economy, which is precisely what the old Corporation claimed to have stood for. Economy meant two different things, however, according to whether you were a Radical or a Tory, and Radical economy was labelled extravagance by the Tories. Economy, to the Tories, meant doing little and paying nobody to do it. Economy, to the Radicals, meant the substitution of salaried officials for amateurs, putting contracts out to tender and awarding them to the lowest bidder, and as time went on the active intervention of the Council in matters of public health. The charities were put into the hands of the Charity Commissioners and of independent trustees, and business standards were applied to all aspects of the city's administration. With one brave gesture the new City Council signalized the change in the city's government by selling the old Corporation plate.[4]

It was not impossible for a manufacturer to become a member of the old Corporation, and George Eliot says that Mr. Vincy was hoping to become Mayor.[5] The manufacturers admitted to the select group of thirty-one members of the Grand Council

---

[1] *Reports Commissioners, 1840,* XXIV, p. 201.

[2] The *Coventry Standard,* 31 July 1840.

[3] The *Coventry Herald* and the *Coventry Standard,* 1 January 1836.

[4] Frederick Smith, *Coventry, Six Hundred Years of Municipal Life,* revised edn., 1946, p. 122.

[5] George Eliot, *Middlemarch,* World's Classics, 1947, p. 100.

seem to have been the 'old manufacturers' of Middlemarch.[1]
But a majority of the members of the old Corporation were
professional men, and men of independent means, bankers,
lawyers, gentlemen, and even members of the landed
aristocracy. When the new City Council took control, the Earl
of Craven resigned his position as the Recorder of the city, while
the old generation of Vales, Carters, and Whitwells gave way to
the Becks, Browetts, Caldicotts, and Ratliffs, all of whom were
new masters in the ribbon trade.[2] So far as the freemen weavers
and watchmakers were concerned, it was doubtful whether the
reform of the municipal corporations had not put the affairs of
the city into the hands of their employers. Certainly it added to
the growing sense of class war, and one weaver had already
observed that

some of those who were most forward in the march of liberalism,
were amongst the first to stamp the rights of labour under foot.[3]

For some years preceding and following the reform local
politics in Coventry were fought with much bitterness. The
members of the old Corporation strove hard to persuade the
House of Lords to act in their defence, and to emasculate
the Bill when it came up from the Commons. When it became
apparent that all their efforts had been in vain, the Mayor,
George Eld, loyally did his best to prepare the way for the new
régime,[4] but some of the others led by Carter acted with some
spite in appointing Thomas Banbury, one of the leaders of the
reform party to the office of Chamberlain.[5] In that office he
would have to collect the fees for the pasturing of the freemen's
horses and cows, without having the compensating prospect of
promotion and pickings in the future. Banbury refused, and the
Corporation applied to the Court of King's Bench for a writ of
mandamus to compel him to take the office, and won its case. It
must have been some consolation to Mr. Banbury when, in

---

[1] ibid, p. 245; and see below, pp. 49-52.   [2] See below pp. 50-52.

[3] The *Coventry Herald*, 29 August 1834.

[4] Eld was a member of the old Corporation, but he seems to have helped it to
begin to put its own house in order before the arrival of the Municipal Corporations
Reform Commissioner, who spoke of a recent improvement in the conduct of the
affairs of the city. *Reports Commissioners, 1835*, XXV, p. 430.

[5] Frederick Smith, *Coventry, Six Hundred Years of Municipal Life*, revised edn., 1946,
pp. 120-1.

November 1836, he was appointed the second Mayor of the reformed city, and the council voted him an official salary of £100 for the year.[1]

The revengeful animosity of the former Town Clerk, however, was not satisfied by his success in making Mr. Banbury brand cattle. Taking advantage of a doubtful clause in the Municipal Corporations Reform Act of 1835, he started an agitation which resulted in the return of the county of Coventry outside the city to the county of Warwickshire in 1842. The wealthy families living in this part of the former North Ward, had been unable to vote at parliamentary elections, and had not been allowed to enjoy the corporate privileges of the city, although they paid the city rates, which were more than double the rates in Warwickshire in this period. By this change they became enfranchised, and ceased to contribute to the upkeep of the city, whose Radical government was thus proved, to the delight of the Tories, to be expensive. As the extinction of the county of Coventry by the Coventry Boundary Act was followed by the loss of the Recorder and of the Quarter Sessions, and the transference of the County Hall to Warwickshire, the city of Coventry was generally felt to have lost much prestige.[2]

Distracted by these artificial conflicts the City Council took several years to take stock of its assets and of its responsibilities. After the return of the county of Coventry outside the city to Warwickshire, the reformers set about the administration of their reduced estate with some zeal and much success, setting an example to the rest of the country. Their first step was to promote an Act of Parliament empowering them to buy land outside the city, by the side of the London road, for a cemetery.[3] This was laid out at their invitation by that great nineteenth century gardener and architect, Joseph Paxton, who was later returned to the House of Commons by the city at a by-election in December 1854. The same Act of Parliament enabled the city to buy the ancient mills which obstructed the Sherbourne and caused it to flood, and to demolish them. When this scheme had been completed, the Ford Street and Lower Ford Street

[1] The *Coventry Standard*, 11 November 1836.

[2] Frederick Smith, *Coventry, Six Hundred Years of Municipal Life*, revised edn., 1946, pp. 123-6; and *Reports Commissioners, 1835*, XXV, p. 429, for the comparative rates of the county and the city.

[3] 7 and 8 Vict., local and personal, c. lxxvi.

area between Coventry and Hillfields could be developed, and the old city joined to the new town.

Having arranged for the decent burial of the dead, the City Council turned its attention to the living, whose first need was for clean water. Another Act of Parliament, passed in 1844, gave the city power to construct an artesian well in Spon End, to build a reservoir, to lay mains through the city, and to carry service pipes to the boundaries of properties.[1] The works were completed in 1847: thereafter, the City Council having plenty of water to spare, and having spent a good deal of money in providing it, encouraged people to use its water, and spent the rates on cleaning the streets with it. By 1851 3,500 out of the total of nearly 8,000 houses in the city were supplied with water from the mains.[2] The gain to the health of the city must have been enormous, because, in the absence of a sewer, many of the private wells in courts and gardens were contaminated as a result of their proximity to the innumerable cesspits of the city.[3]

The sewer, however, followed hard upon the heels of the water supply, for Coventry was quick to adopt the Health of Towns Act of 1848,[4] and to establish a Local Board of Health. This was simply the City Council meeting in a different capacity, and the Local Board met for the first time in August 1849. The following year the city was surveyed by the Ordnance Survey, and plans were made for the construction of an arterial sewer, and for the connexion of every street to the main artery. The Board appointed a full-time inspector, Mr. Greatorex, to suppress offensive privies and cesspits, and, so far as drains were concerned, by the mid-fifties Coventry was well on the way to becoming a model city.[5]

Greatorex was also responsible for seeing that the new building regulations laid down by the Board were complied with. The regulations concerned the height of rooms, the width of streets, and the separation of buildings. A two story building, for instance, must not be placed within forty feet, and a three

[1] 7 & 8 Vict., local and personal, c. lvi.

[2] B. Poole, *Coventry, Its History and Antiquities*, 1869, pp. 342-3, William Ranger, *Report to the General Board of Health*, &c., 1849, p. 10 seq., and the *Coventry Herald*, 1 August 1851.

[3] See William Ranger, *Report to the General Board of Health*, &c., 1849, p. 16.

[4] 11 & 12 Vict., public, c. lxiii.

[5] The records of the Local Board of Health are in the City Record Office.

story building within sixty feet of another building. These standards corresponded to the generally accepted practice of the day and their object was to exclude the worse class of builder, not to stimulate the better. The standard for roads was that they should be forty feet wide, including footpaths, and Yardley Street, constructed just before the Local Board came into existence, meets the prescribed standard, and looks exactly like Vernon Street, which was constructed shortly afterwards.

The standards that were imposed were the standards already accepted by the capitalists who were investing their money in houses, and by the builders themselves. This is an interesting point. Regulation was new, and the standards had to be such that they would not discourage investors, for Coventry needed new buildings. All that the Board could do, therefore, was to set a minimum standard, and to level up to it. The skimpier builder must be made to realize that it was he, and not the Board, that was being unreasonable. In this way, with public opinion behind it, the Board set to work. All building plans had to be submitted for its consideration, and those that were below standard were rejected.[1] Most of the rejected plans were referred to a General Works Committee, which often undertook to explain to the builder where his plans had gone wrong, and how they could be amended. Many of the plans that were rejected at first were passed later, after alteration.

By the 1850's then, the problems of public health were being tackled vigorously. The death rate fell within a few years from 27 to 23 per thousand—or, as Charles Bray put it, in a population of 40,000, 160 lives had been saved every year.[2] But while the population continued to grow, from the 27,000 of 1831 towards the 41,000 of 1861, the old and original problem remained, affecting both public health and the prosperity of the town, of the enclosure of the Lammas and Michaelmas lands. The reconstruction of the Holyhead road, the construction of the railway, and the provision of the cemetery, had all necessitated the enclosure of small parts of these lands. On each occasion compensation had been paid into the freemen's seniority, or pension fund. But the mass of the lands remained, and the great obstacle to their enclosure was now the question

---

[1] About a quarter of all those submitted in the 1850's.

[2] Charles Bray, *Phases of Opinion*, &c., 1884, p. 51.

of compensation. Had the freemen, in return for the surrender of their rights of pasture, a right to compensation in money only, or in land? Should the freemen obtain compensation in land, they need only wait till their land was built over to become exceedingly rich.

Charles Bray made a serious attempt to resolve the deadlock in 1843. He says that he tried to effect the enclosure on the basis of the freemen's receiving one-third of the value of the land in money. He obtained the signatures of two-thirds of the freemen, and encouraged by his success the City Council prepared to apply for the appropriate Act of Parliament. Opinion now swung back; the freemen reverted to the idea of compensation in land; the *bona fide* owners of the land would not agree, the Bill was opposed, and after £500 had been spent on either side, it was thrown out.[1]

The setback was a long one. Bray himself had become unpopular with both sides.

At one time I could scarcely go from my house to business without being abused, and sometimes pelted. Going home one night when it was very dark, I heard a knot of workmen discussing the question. It was asked what *I* wanted with the enclosure. One repeated the old tale that I was in the interest of the landowners: another said that I was rich, and that I wanted the land round my house for a park: another that they were both wrong, for I was what they call a 'pheelanthropist'. 'What's that?', they asked. 'Why', said the man, 'it's a man who acts from no motive at all.'[2]

On this issue Bray showed more perseverance than usual, and, in the 1850's, a doubt arising whether the lands might not be enclosed under the Health of Towns Act, the freemen, realizing that the writing was on the wall, decided to close for the best terms they could get, and themselves petitioned the Enclosure Commissioners to take the matter up.[3] Assistant Commissioner J. J. Rawlinson came down to Coventry; the lands were surveyed; it was decided rightly or wrongly that the freemen were entitled to compensation in land; and when the enclosure awards were made in 1860 and 1875, the freemen received seven-twenty-fourths of the Lammas and one-fifth of the

[1] Charles Bray, *Phases of Opinion*, &c., 1884, pp. 82-83.   [2] ibid, p. 84.
[3] Under the 'General Enclosure Act', 7 & 8 Vict., public, c. xviii.

Michaelmas lands, or 273 acres, as their share.[1] The constricted city surrounded by untouchable fields had disappeared.

Meantime, before the enclosure awards, building went on in the few available places. A majority of the two thousand houses built between 1841 and 1861 were built in Hillfields, the weavers' new town. But an Act of Parliament of 1845 authorized the sale of some of the lands of Sir Thomas White's charity,[2] and as a result, Chapelfields became available for building at the other end of the town, beyond Spon End. In the 1850's this was already becoming the watchmakers' suburb. At the same time a number of middle class houses were being built in the south of the city in the Marquis of Hertford's park, while the new and miscellaneous suburb of Earlsdon was growing up on the south-west of the city outside the city boundary, helped by the fact that apprentices living in Earlsdon could win the freedom of the city.[3]

The new houses helped to relieve the congestion in the crowded courts of the old city. In doing so they contributed to a division in the class structure. For the last hundred years the working men of Coventry had been crowding into these courts. Good workmen and bad workmen had rubbed shoulders in the same court, or lived in adjacent courts. Now, however, with the opening of the new suburbs, it was the better class of weavers and other working men, corresponding closely to the freemen, who were extricating themselves from the old city. In their new quarters there was air and light, and though many of the roads were still badly made up, the houses were well built, and there were gardens and allotments. The standard of living of those who could remove to Hillfields, or Chapelfields, or Earlsdon was going up, while the old courts became slums, and those who lived in them, degenerated into slum dwellers.

Everything conspired against the inhabitants of the older parts of the city. The air in their courts had always been foul, but as long as the city was hemmed in by open country, they were never far away from the fresh air. After this period, when the city began to expand on all sides, and before these courts

---

[1] Charles Bray, *Phases of Opinion*, &c., 1884, pp. 84-85. There is a slightly different account in B. Poole, *Coventry, Its History and Antiquities*, 1869, pp. 355-7. But Poole would not have been likely to refer to Bray's part in these proceedings.

[2] 8 & 9 Vict., private, c. xvii.

[3] See the Register of Apprentices' Indentures in the City Record Office.

could be removed by slum clearance and by bombing, they were cut off from the countryside by half a mile or a mile of new buildings—a disadvantage that the bicycle and the tram could not altogether offset. Furthermore, the regulations laid down by the Local Board of Health, which were intended to preserve the working classes from the evils of bad housing, at first served only to emphasize the differences between the old and the new areas, for these regulations could only be applied to new houses—not to old ones. Thanks to the Local Board, the weaver who could get to Hillfields in the 1850's was guaranteed a decent house. But the Board could do nothing for the weaver who could not escape from the old city to the suburb.

Now that the break-out had begun, the free play of economic and social forces, in which the nineteenth century believed so strongly, was thus tending towards a separation of classes. This separation was likely to be permanent, because, other things being equal, there was more opportunity to make good in Hillfields than in the old city. So that when the time came for the next move, it would be the same people, or their children, who would move into new houses. For some families life would become a succession of new houses, and for others a succession of third- and fourth-hand ones. The better class of artisans would be ready to abandon Hillfields itself when the time came. Meantime, Hillfields was to become the home, not only of so many of the upper class of freemen weavers, but of the cottage factory, while the old city was to become the home of the lower class of weavers and of the factory. There were exceptions to this rule, and the process was in any case a gradual one. Over a period of thirty years, however, from 1830 to 1860, the working class in Coventry was divided into two. This naturally complicated the relations of the working classes with their employers, and the relations of both workmen and employers with public opinion, to which both sides appealed during industrial disputes.

III

THE ORGANIZATION OF THE RIBBON TRADE IN THE 1830's

THE EXTENT OF THE TRADE

IN Western Europe English ribbons were in competition with those of Lyons, St. Etienne, and Basle. In the United Kingdom Coventry shared the production of ribbons with Derby, Leek, and Congleton, and the city was connected, in so far as the ribbon trade was a part of the silk trade, with the towns weaving broad silks—Spitalfields, Manchester, and Macclesfield.[1] From 1768 to 1826 the import of foreign ribbons had been prohibited, but extensive smuggling, and a growing belief in free trade had since led to the substitution of a protective tariff, which in 1830 stood at 25 per cent. Consequently, on the English market, the French and the Swiss now enjoyed a large share of the upper and upper-middle class trade in fancy (or figured) ribbons, while Coventry supplied the middle and lower class trade in fancy ribbons, and together with Derby, Leek, and Congleton, supplied the whole of England with plain ones.[2]

[1] For a general account of the silk trades see F. Warner, *Silk Industry of the United Kingdom*, 1921.

[2] *Reports Commissioners, 1840*, XXIV, p. 31. The page references to this volume are to the pages of the volume, and not to those of the report.

The report was the work of Joseph Fletcher, who, in his capacity as Assistant Commissioner to the Unemployed Handloom Weavers' Commission, came to the city for six weeks towards the end of 1838. Fletcher was only twenty-five years old at the time: educated as a barrister, with leanings towards Utilitarianism, he made a brilliant investigator and statistician, and he became a founder member of the Royal Statistical Society, and a strong advocate of national education before he died in 1852, at the early age of thirty-nine.

Fletcher not only communicated his enthusiasm to Charles Bray, who collected some statistics for him, but to the weavers of Coventry, some of the most 'reliable' of whom went round every ward making a census of the weavers, their families, their looms, their masters, and their work. Consequently Fletcher's blue book is remarkable both for its detail, and for its reliability.

Even the Tory *Standard*, which on 14 December 1838, alleged that the whole inquiry was being conducted in order to prove two pet Whig theories, the necessity for free trade and for a system of national education, spoke appreciatively of Fletcher himself.

The silk was imported from France, Italy, Turkey, and the Far East, by merchants in London and Manchester. Some silk was imported ready thrown, but the rest was imported raw, and put out to be thrown before being sent to the Coventry manufacturer in the hank. The manufacturer had to have the silk dyed and woven before sending the finished ribbons to a dealer for distribution among the retail traders. No manufacturer dealt directly with a retailer.

The trade fluctuated severely according to the season. The new designs had to reach the shops during the spring in order to be worn during the summer. For the producer, therefore, the summer was a slack period in which old stocks were sold and new designs prepared. In addition to the annual variations in trade according to the season, there were the less regular cyclical variations according to the general state of trade.[1] Other completely unpredictable variations took place on account of changes of fashion. The death of the king or queen would send the whole nation into mourning, and the demand for the plain black ribbons woven at Derby would increase at the expense of the fancy ribbons woven at Coventry.[2] Sometimes, without warning, ladies would give up wearing ribbons for the year, and ornament their dresses with beads or feathers instead.

The first feature of a trade of this kind was a pool of casual labour, which could be brought into employment when things were busy, and laid off again when they were slack. Since its establishment in Coventry in the early eighteenth century,[3] the ribbon weaving had spread, in successive periods of prosperity, among the wives of the colliers in the villages to the north and north-east of the city.[4] By the 1830's the trade extended to the 'frontier' with the stocking knitting of Leicestershire—another trade carried on mostly in the home and in the same conditions. If one trade was slack and the other busy, an attempt would be made to change the frontier between them, but these attempts did not survive the return of 'normal' conditions, and throughout the nineteenth century the frontier corresponded exactly to the boundary between the two counties.[5] In this way Coventry had become the centre of a weaving area in which 13,000 looms

---

[1] *Reports Commissioners, 1840*, XXIV, pp. 50, 70.

[2] The *Coventry Herald*, 30 April 1830.

[3] *Reports Commissioners, 1840*, XXIV, p. 19.   [4] ibid, p. 21.   [5] ibid, p. 70.

supported about 30,000 people.[1] Included in this area, but independently organized, were the half-dozen small masters of Bedworth, and the four larger ones of Nuneaton.[2] All the villages between Coventry and Nuneaton had become subordinate to these weaving centres, Hartshill and Chilvers Coton being reckoned with Nuneaton, Bulkington with Bedworth, and Ansty, Shilton, Sowe, and Exhall with Coventry. Foleshill, just to the north of Coventry, was still a part of the county of the city in the 1830's, and seems to have enjoyed a privileged position and to have belonged more to the city than to the country trade, with male labour and wages paid according to the list of prices.[3] These villages were an essential, but the least regarded part of the weaving trade. They were given work only when the city had more orders than it could manage, and they were the first to be laid off when there was a recession. Last in, first out, they lived in almost complete subjection to the city which exploited them, and kept them permanently on the margin of employment.[4] The opposition of the great landlords, determined to prevent anything which might lead to an increased poor rate, was said to have prevented the weaving from spreading into the villages to the south and west of the city, which remained purely agricultural.[5]

THE TECHNICAL PROCESSES AND THE DISTRIBUTION OF LOOMS

In the early 1830's the need for better supervision was already leading to the introduction of the factory system in advance of the use of steam power.[6] All the country weavers, and a majority of the city weavers still worked at home, but these domestic weavers and the manufacturers who employed them were frequently involved in disputes about the embezzlement of silk, and the quality of the silk given out. Furthermore the domestic weavers were accustomed to take things easily at

---

1 ibid, Table I, p. 28, for the number of looms. The population of the entire area was greater, but 30,000 is a reasonable estimate of the number of people supported by the ribbon trade at this time.

2 ibid, p. 51.   3 ibid, p. 30.

4 ibid, p. 54. Notice, too, George Eliot's reference in *Middlemarch*, World's Classics, 1947, p. 348, to Mr. Vincy as 'one of those who suck the life out of the wretched handloom weavers of Tipton and Freshitt'.

5 ibid, p. 21.   6 ibid, p. 62.

the beginning of the week, and to work excessively long hours towards the end, spoiling their work because they were tired.[1] From the manufacturer's point of view there was already much to be said in favour of factories, where men and women worked regular hours, at a steady pace throughout the week, and in 1838 twenty-seven manufacturers employed weavers in small loom-shops or factories.[2]

Before the dyed silk could be woven into ribbons, the weavers, who were of both sexes, had to 'wind' it, to 'prepare the warps', and to 'fill the quills'.[3] Winding the silk meant taking it out of the hank, and winding it round a drum to obtain the even tension which made all the difference to the quality of the warps—the threads which form the length of a ribbon. The preparation of the warps was a matter of some nicety, and it commonly took a whole morning to fit them to a loom.[4] Having fitted the warps to the loom, the weaver was ready to pass his shuttle to and fro between them. The silk was carried in the shuttles on quills, which had to be filled with silk before the weaving could begin. These preparatory tasks were often the work of women and children, and account for the fact that there were more people engaged in the weaving trade than there were looms. In the factories, at least, these tasks were now performed efficiently, according to the principle of the division of labour.

The acquisition of specialized skills had not yet led, through the rationalization of processes, to any very ambitious use of machinery, and compared with the cotton trades the silk trades were still primitive. The apparatus used in dyeing, winding, warping, and quill filling was rudimentary, and these remained exclusively hand operations. It was only in the weaving itself that men looked for hand labour to be superseded by power driven machinery. But here too progress had been slow, for silk is more delicate than cotton. The original loom had been the 'single hand loom', weaving one breadth of ribbon at a time. For the weaving of ordinary plain ribbons, this had begun to be

---

[1] *Reports Commissioners, 1840*, XXIV, pp. 301-2.   [2] ibid, Table X, p. 63.

[3] For these processes see, *Reports Commissioners, 1840*, XXIV, p. 52, and the article on 'The Ribbon Trade' in *The Resources, Products, and Industrial History of Birmingham and the Midland Hardware District*, ed. S. Timmins, 1866.

[4] When there were disputes between the different branches of the trade, the most obvious injury one weaver could do to another was to cut the warps out of his loom.

superseded about 1770 by the 'Dutch engine loom'. The word
engine must not be taken to mean the use of power; for all the
Dutch engine loom did was to enable the weaver to weave
several plain ribbons at once. The new invention did not put the
old single hand looms out of business altogether, because the
Dutch engine loom could not be used for fancy ribbons, which
had still to be woven in the old way.[1]

The weavers themselves determined that women should not
be allowed to use the engine loom, and this prohibition,
enforced by custom, not law, effectively prevented the engine
loom spreading to the country districts, where the weavers were
nearly all women.[2] Although the restriction was sound, in so far
as it resisted the dangerous tendency of the times to substitute
female for male labour, it was unjust, because it made the
country weaver more than ever the poor relation of his or her
counterpart in the town. In 1834 the single hand weavers of
Nuneaton complained that the continuous improvement of the
Coventry engine looms had reduced them to a state in which no
change could be for the worse.[3]

The Dutch engine loom had been challenged in its turn by
Jacquard's invention in 1795, of a system of needles operated by
punched cards, which made it possible to weave fancy ribbons
in quantity, with several breadths in the loom at the same time.
The Jacquard loom, therefore, combined the advantage of the
Dutch engine loom of quantity production with the advantage
of the single hand loom that it could weave figures. Although
the Jacquard loom spread slowly, and was not much used in
Coventry until the late 1820's,[4] the result was the gradual
disappearance of the Dutch engine loom, and a further
reduction in the number of single hand looms. The Jacquard
loom was ultimately to kill the Dutch engine loom, because
there was nothing the Dutch engine loom could do that the
Jacquard could not do better, but it was never to kill the
single hand loom, which thus outlasted its original competitor.
This was because there was a limit to the number of threads
with which the Jacquard could cope, and the very highest
classes of fancy ribbons, tartans and exhibition ribbons, had

1 *Reports Commissioners, 1840*, XXIV, p. 21.   2 ibid, pp. 49, 60.

3 The *Coventry Herald*, 10 January 1834.

4 *Reports Commissioners, 1840*, XXIV, p. 25.

still to be woven on the single hand loom.[1] Already, however, by the 1830's, any single hand loom that was not engaged on these higher classes of work, must have been bringing in but little reward for long hours of labour because of the competition of the more advanced looms.

Machinery is one thing and power another. To drive the Jacquard loom by power must have been the ambition of every budding Arkwright in the trade. But the power loom, when it came, was at first more suitable for plain ribbons than fancy, and it was in consequence adopted more readily in Derby than in Coventry. The first steam factory in Coventry was not built until 1831, in Mr. Beck's yard, and it had not been working long before it was burnt down by a mob of weavers frightened for their employment. Gutteridge, who was at that time only a boy, says that he had an intense desire to see the new machinery which dispensed with manual labour, and

I went to the ill-fated factory with one of the men employed there, and it was while I was inspecting the looms, absorbed with the beauty and simplicity of their arrangement, that the rioters commenced to demolish them, to pile the broken pieces on a heap of shavings, and deliberately set fire to them.[2]

Meanwhile, Mr. Beck had barricaded himself in the attic, and when the fire spread and the flames reached him, he had to let himself out of the window on the end of a blanket. He was caught by the mob as he tried to escape over a wall, dragged forth, and set on a donkey with his face to the tail, amidst the yells and execrations of the crowd. The weavers began to parade the donkey through the streets before the Magistrates had time to call out the soldiers to restore order and rescue the unfortunate manufacturer.[3]

Gutteridge's father must have been glad that his son was not involved in the subsequent trial of Burbury and Spark, the ringleaders. Vengeance was Mr. Beck's, but the victory for the time being lay with the weavers. For six years no further attempt was made to introduce steam power to Coventry, and it was left to

---

[1] *The Resources, Products, and Industrial History of Birmingham and the Midland Hardware District*, ed. S. Timmins, 1866, article on 'The Ribbon Trade'.

[2] Joseph Gutteridge, *Lights and Shadows*, &c., 1893, p. 33.

[3] The *Coventry Herald*, 11 November 1831.

the rival manufacturers at Derby to develop the power loom.[1] Finally, when these North Midland masters began to enter the Coventry trade in fancy ribbons, a syndicate was formed in Coventry, in 1836, to divide the risks and profits of constructing and operating a power driven factory. The factory was built; the members of the syndicate fell out; several other attempts were made to erect steam factories, and of the fifty-three power looms in the city in 1838 forty-five were operated by Mr. Day, and the rest by Mr. Cope.[2]

When Joseph Fletcher, the Assistant Commissioner to the Unemployed Handloom Weavers Commission came to Coventry in 1838, he found that after nearly seventy years of competition between the different types of loom, and the different classes of weavers, there remained over 7,000 single hand looms in the country districts, and only 130 in the city. The 3,504 remaining Dutch engine looms were situated entirely in the city and Foleshill, and out of the total of 2,228 Jacquard looms, 1,678 were to be found in Coventry and Foleshill, 320 in Bedworth, and 200 in Nuneaton.[3]

THE CLASSES ENGAGED IN THE TRADE: THE MASTERS

At the end of the eighteenth century the trade had been managed by ten or twelve merchant manufacturers. These men kept warehouses in London and in Coventry, and the capital required to enter the trade was so great that there were few changes.[4] These were the 'old manufacturers' of Middlemarch,[5] masters of their trade, known to each other, known to their connexions in London, and known by and large to the weavers of Coventry. Under them the trade seems to have been quietly governed, and there were few strikes.

Associated with the manufacturers were the 'undertakers', who collected the silk at the manufacturers' warehouses in Coventry, and took it away to be woven. Some of the undertakers had small loom shops of their own, where they employed half a dozen looms, while others simply handed the silk over to the weavers in their own homes. When the undertaker returned the completed ribbons to the warehouse in Coventry, the

---

[1] *Reports Commissioners, 1840*, XXIV, p. 67.   [2] ibid, pp. 27, 67-69.

[3] ibid, Table I, p. 28.   [4] ibid, p. 49.

[5] George Eliot, *Middlemarch*, World's Classics, 1947, p. 245.

manufacturer sent them on to his second warehouse in London for distribution to the wholesalers. The custom of the trade awarded one-third of the manufacturer's price for the ribbons to the undertaker, whose expenses were often considerable, and two-thirds to the weaver.[1] Under this system any diligent and thrifty weaver might hope to become an undertaker. At forty or fifty years of age he would still have the best years of his life to come, for, with his children grown up, and half a dozen looms in his shop, he could rent a good house, and enjoy his pint or two of best ale in the evening.[2] Further than this he could not hope to rise, for the gap between the undertakers and the manufacturers was much too wide for him to cross. Anyone with a little capital could enter the trade as an undertaker, but no man of little capital could dominate the trade as a master.[3]

The trade had, however, been turned upside down towards the end of the Napoleonic wars, during a boom period known as the 'big purl time', when many weavers were away fighting the French, and there was an unprecedented demand for ribbons. The wholesalers in London, disregarding their established trade connexions with the old manufacturers of Coventry, had discovered that they could get their ribbons woven more cheaply by going to Coventry themselves, and making their own arrangements with the undertakers, a large number of whom must have become small masters overnight.[4] The trade had in fact been thrown open to competition, and with a little credit anyone could enter it. The London merchants now gave five months credit for silk, and the small masters could have the silk dyed, woven into ribbons, and sold to the wholesale houses for cash, three months before their bills became due. The ten or twelve old masters had now to contend with forty or fifty smaller masters of a new kind,[5] while the old-fashioned undertaker disappeared, except in the country districts, where the old-fashioned looms continued to be worked in the old-fashioned way, and where, in the 1830's, there were still approximately 1,000 undertakers, or one undertaker to every seven looms.[6]

In 1838 there were no fewer than seventy manufacturers in

---

[1] *Reports Commissioners, 1840*, XXIV, p. 49.

[2] The *Coventry Standard*, 22 February 1850.

[3] *Reports Commissioners, 1840*, XXIV, p. 49.

[4] ibid, pp. 50, 214-15.   [5] ibid, pp. 50-51.   [6] ibid, p. 53.

the city employing under ten looms each, and thirty-five more employing between 10 and 100. On the other hand there were still twelve manufacturers employing over 100 looms each, and the largest manufacturer of all, Mr. Cope, actually employed over 400.[1] Socially, the old master manufacturers were still able to hold their own:

there were nice distinctions of rank in Middlemarch; and though old manufacturers could not any more than dukes be connected with none but equals, they were conscious of an inherent social superiority which was defined with great nicety in practice, though hardly expressible theoretically.[2]

The standards of life of these masters were high, and George Eliot tells us that Mr. Vincy spent money on coursing, on his cellar, and on giving dinners, while Mrs. Vincy

had those running accounts with tradespeople, which give a cheerful sense of getting everything one wants without any question of payment.[3]

Men of this stamp, who had kept a good house for three generations, could afford to be generous to their weavers, and indeed both their consciences and the sense of honour of the town demanded it.[4]

The new, small masters were not acceptable socially, though some of them were able to make a success of business. But these men of little capital had to live upon their wits. They took advantage of the repeal of the Elizabethan apprenticeship regulations in 1814: they began to employ women at the engine loom: they instituted half-pay apprenticeships, which were really no apprenticeships at all; and the weavers complained bitterly of the exactions and petty tyranny of men who, a few years before, had been no better in situation than themselves.[5] The Tory *Standard* took some pleasure in pointing out that it was the journeyman master, the manufacturer from hand to mouth, who was foremost to clip down wages, and to resort to all sorts of oppression towards the weavers.[6] As the years went by and the

---

[1] *Reports Commissioners, 1840*, XXIV, p. 51.

[2] George Eliot, *Middlemarch*, World's Classics, 1947, p. 245.

[3] ibid, p. 243.   [4] *Reports Commissioners, 1840*, XXIV, p. 216.

[5] The *Coventry Standard*, 7 August 1840.   [6] ibid, 3 September 1858.

City Council was substituted for the Corporation, some of these men were to become influential in the affairs of the city, and were to be chosen to sit upon the Bench.

Nothing had used to be so respectable in a manufacturing town as to be an old manufacturer. But the ribbon trade had now been invaded by a crowd of petty masters whose only scruple was to buy in the cheapest and sell in the dearest market. The conduct of the old masters towards their weavers had not been ungenerous, being based upon the assumption that the weaver ought at least to be able to live by his labour. The new masters were different: like Mr. J. Jenkins, they preferred to employ labour upon the same principle that they would purchase goods, i.e. to pay as little for it as possible.[1] Great changes were to follow upon their arrival in the trade. In one way only were the new masters and the old masters alike: neither seem to have left records of their businesses.

THE CLASSES ENGAGED IN THE TRADE: THE WEAVERS

In Coventry, as in England, there was a strong popular prejudice against working in factories. Consequently, the 'first-hand journeymen', or outdoor weavers, who worked in their own homes, were generally believed to be superior to the factory hands. Between these two classes there floated, in the 1830's, a class of 'journeymen's journeymen', working either for the first-hand journeymen, or in the factories, whose ambition it was to become first-hand journeymen themselves, but who were likely, if they fell on evil days, to subside into the ranks of the factory hands. The first-hand journeymen did, and the factory hands did not, regard the possession of property (a loom) as the basis of marriage.[2]

Much the most important of these classes, which if it was not peculiar to Coventry, was at least peculiarly strong in Coventry, was the class of first-hand journeymen. These were unquestionably working men, but they were working men with bourgeois virtues. They had 'a stake in society': many of them were freemen, and they were therefore, as a class, the controlling factor in parliamentary elections. They might have been forgiven for thinking that they could make themselves heard at

[1] *Reports Committees, 1835*, XIII, p. 273, para. 4233.
[2] *Reports Commissioners, 1840*, XXIV, Chapter II, ss. 2, 3, pp. 55-65.

Westminster, though as a matter of fact they were mistaken. They were men who paid high rents for, or even owned their houses. Their looms were their own, and though most of them worked for manufacturers, forty of them in 1838 were in business on their own account, swelling the number of little masters, with 121 looms between them.[1] Most of the first-hands saved money, and many of them, like Gutteridge, had interests outside their work.

In the city and its suburbs, there were in 1838 1,828 of these loom-owning first-hand journeymen working for the manu-facturers. 1,614 of them were men, and 214 women.[2] They owned, between them, 3,967 looms, of which no fewer than 3,145 were worked by members of their own families. Journeymen's journeymen no doubt worked the rest. These 1,828 weavers with their 3,967 looms supported families of 6,796 people.[3] In a total population of 30,000, this was no small percentage, and the independent spirit of Coventry in this period was very largely based upon the independent spirit of these 1,828 first-hand journeymen.

The class of journeymen's journeymen was, on the other hand, much smaller. There were 1,225 of them, 878 men and 347 women, and they and the families they supported came to a total of 2,480 people. Of these 1,225 men and women, 852 worked for first-hand journeymen, and 373 in factories.[4] No figures are known for the factory working population, but the twenty-seven manufacturers with factories or loom shops had a total of 598 looms,[5] and there must have been several hundred permanent factory operatives in addition to the 373 journey-men's journeymen who were working in factories.[6]

THE REGULATION OF THE TRADE BY MASTERS AND MEN: THE LIST OF PRICES

Much the most striking feature of the city trade in the 1820's and 1830's was the continued devotion of both masters and men to the payment of wages according to a published 'list of prices'. The prices paid were such as to enable the weaver to live

---

[1] *Reports Commissioners, 1840*, XXIV, Table X, p. 63.

[2] ibid, Table VI, p. 57.   [3] ibid, Table VII, p. 58.

[4] ibid, Table VIII, p. 59.   [5] ibid, Table X, p. 63.

[6] ibid, Table VIII, p. 59.

comfortably without having to go to the parish for supplementation. It was generally agreed that, in the language of the time, no 'honourable' manufacturer would offer to pay, and no 'honourable' weaver would accept, anything less than this living wage. Everyone knew, therefore, that if all men were honourable, there would be no possibility of the trade being disturbed through disputes about wages. Time and again both the manufacturers and the weavers reiterated their conviction that most of their number were honourable. Unfortunately, experience kept on revealing that some at least were not, and that even the normally honourable man might be tempted by circumstances to be dishonourable once in a while, to the injury of everyone else.[1]

There were three main causes of disputes over list prices. In the first place the introduction of a new and more productive loom made it difficult to maintain the list of prices for work done on the older looms. This was to become an important source of friction in the 1850's.[2] In the second place, it was impossible to draw up a list of prices covering all the many varieties of ribbon woven in Coventry, some of which were woven in small quantities. There was a recognized price for each width and quality of plain ribbons, and for the more popular fancy ribbons, and it was customary to pay extra for the other fancy ribbons according to the amount of extra work involved.[3] Naturally this left plenty of room for dispute.

In the third place, the dishonourable masters, who corresponded closely at this period to the small masters, were tempted to pay below list prices because of the competition for work. The trade being a fluctuating one and hardly a year passing without a recession, there were nearly always men idle, who were prepared to take out work below the list prices. The weavers argued that if there were no list, and there were 101 men available for the work for which 100 were needed, the one man, being thrown out of employment, must offer his services lower than one of the others, and that

that man would soon be reduced to the circumstances of his

---

[1] e.g. the *Coventry Herald*, 2 January 1824, 18 April 1828, and 23 September 1831. The *Coventry Standard*, 10 March 1837, and 21 April 1837.

[2] See below, Chapter VII, p. 113.

[3] *Reports Commissioners, 1840*, XXIV, lists on pp. 252-6.

competitor. Thus only one surplus labourer would have the effect of diminishing the price of labour of the whole community.[1]

A good deal of argument went on at this time, as to whether the dishonourable weaver who accepted, or the dishonourable master who paid too low a wage, was most to blame. Most people would have agreed with Mr. Cope, the largest manufacturer, that the evil did not rest so much with the operative as with the manufacturer, because the weaver took the work from necessity while the manufacturer offered it from avarice.[2]

The worst feature of this state of affairs was that the bad master was always tending to pull the good master down to his own level. Just as the competition for work among the weavers was always tending to make dishonourable weavers of them all, so the 'more honest part of the masters were always being compelled, in self-defence, to reduce their prices to the same level'.[3] Recognizing this fact, the good masters and the good men were always looking for ways of combining to try to impose their own standards upon the minority who flouted them. In this they were greatly helped by the fact that at no time did they have any difficulty in agreeing upon what constituted a just wage. At the beginning of the nineteenth century the price of labour was perfectly well known to all, whether manufacturers, undertakers, or journeyhands,[4] and as late as 1829-30, provided the representatives of the two sides could meet, they could negotiate either a reduction or an increase in list prices without coming to blows.[5]

The first serious attempt to overthrow the agreed list of prices followed the change in the management of the trade at the end of the Napoleonic wars.[6] Since the better manufacturers shared the weavers' desire for stable prices, the two sides met at the Castle Inn on 28 September 1816 to draw up a new list.[7] This list was for the first time published, but it was not long

---

[1] The *Coventry Standard*, 5 August 1840.

[2] The *Coventry Herald*, 2 October 1829.

[3] ibid, 18 April 1828. *Reports Commissioners, 1840*, XXIV, p. 248.

[4] *Reports Commissioners, 1840*, XXIV, p. 50.

[5] The *Coventry Herald*, 10 September 1830.   [6] See above p. 50.

[7] George Hall, *Prize Essay, on the most advisable mode of establishing a board of Conciliation and Arbitration with a view to prevent strikes, and otherwise to establish and maintain Confidence between Manufacturers and Weavers*, 1861, p. 11, and *Reports Commissioners, 1840*, XXIV, p. 216.

before the small masters again refused to pay list prices. The weavers organized an association to help those who were out of work and to save them from the temptation to accept work at reduced prices,[1] while the masters combined with the men to petition Parliament to pass an Act for the regulation of the wages in the ribbon trade in Coventry, on the lines of the Spitalfields Act of 1773.[2] This was indeed to swim against the tide of legislative wisdom, which had already set strongly in favour of treating labour as a commodity like any other, and Parliament repealed the Spitalfields Act itself in 1825.

Notwithstanding the unfavourable attitude of the Parliament at Westminster, the citizens of Coventry, and handloom weavers everywhere, continued to press for the protection of wages by law.[3] In 1828 a meeting in Coventry passed a resolution urging the government to pass an Act

to empower the majority of the manufacturers and weavers, convened by special meeting, to make a scale which should be valid and binding upon all, till altered by future agreement.[4]

Fielden made a similar proposal in a Bill intended to apply to weavers all over the country in 1835, and as late as 1838 another meeting was held to press for the establishment of a 'Board of Trade' for the regulation of wages in Coventry.[5] Long before this, however, the manufacturers and the weavers must have known that they stood no chance of making their wishes law. Indeed, from the moment the troubles about the list began, at the end of the Napoleonic wars, the two sides had turned to union as the best alternative method of saving the list.

In 1819 the infringements of the list brought on a short but

[1] Called the City of Coventry Weavers Provident Union for Trade and Burial, *Reports Commissioners, 1840*, XXIV, p. 215.

[2] See, *Reports Committees, 1818*, IX, and *Reports Commissioners, 1840*, XXIV, p. 217. The Spitalfields Act, 13 Geo. III, c. 68, repealed by 5 Geo. IV, c. 66, encouraged a Committee of the masters and a Committee of the men to make their own bargain collectively, and made it possible for the Magistrates to enforce this bargain upon all individually. Only when the masters and men had failed to agree on the collective bargain, could the Magistrates determine the wages to be paid. See *Reports Commissioners, 1840*, XXIV, pp. 219-23, and J. H. Clapham, 'The Spitalfields Acts', *Economic Journal*, XXVI, 1916.

[3] See *Reports Committees, 1834*, X, pp. 48, 49.

[4] The *Coventry Herald*, 18 April 1828.

[5] The *Coventry Standard*, 14 September 1838.

successful strike. The Magistrates arranged a meeting between the two sides, a new list was drawn up, signed, and published, and the weavers and their masters then united in a single union for the protection of the list.

A large fund was subscribed to aid in this purpose, under the patronage of Mr. Ellice . . . M.P. for the city, and deposited in Messrs. Troughtons' Bank, Mr. Charles Lilley, a retired manufacturer, acting as Treasurer. In April 1820 this sum amounted to . . . £16,000.[1]

Unfortunately, the Combination Laws being still in existence, the organization, despite the patronage of Mr. Ellice, was clearly illegal, and following an adverse verdict at the Assizes, the organization was broken up, and the funds handed over to the Street Commissioners to be employed in paving the streets.[2]

When the Combination Laws were repealed in 1824 and 1825, the time had passed for the two sides to join forces in a single union, because many of the masters were by that time unwilling to co-operate either with their own class or with the weavers. For the next few years the weavers alone had a union, which attempted to enforce the list of prices unilaterally. The weavers' difficulty was that they had no corresponding body of manufacturers with which to negotiate, and they complained that while they conducted their affairs in the open, the masters were acting in secret.[3] The various techniques which the weavers' union now developed for bringing the masters to the conference table, were to serve them well until the middle of the century.

So long as the list was kept, the weavers' organization remained inert, and there were at this period no regular weekly contributions to the union. In a town as small and crowded as Coventry this was no handicap to their organization, for every weaver could be summoned to a union meeting at a few hours notice. Thanks to the Lammas lands labour troubles could not be overcome by the expedient, practised in Manchester and elsewhere, of bringing labour (Irish probably) from outside. The moment a dispute arose, the weavers called a meeting of the

---

[1] George Hall, *Prize Essay*, 1851, p. 13.

[2] ibid, p. 14, and *Reports Commissioners, 1840*, XXIV, p. 234.

[3] The *Coventry Herald*, 8 May 1829.

first-hand journeymen, or of the factory hands, whichever were involved. These meetings generally took place at one of the many public houses within the city, but every so often, when feelings were running high, the weavers adjourned to the Hill and Hollow Close, outside the city, where rash words could be uttered with impunity.[1]

At these meetings it was almost always decided that the hands in the employment of the offending manufacturer should strike work. Meantime, the weavers employed in that branch of the trade by other manufacturers would contribute so much per week per loom to support them, and to keep them off the parish, in order that the men on strike, if they were freemen, should not forfeit their parliamentary votes. At the same meeting arrangements would be made to go the round of the wards to collect the subscriptions.[2] The weavers were greatly helped in these tactics by the attitude of the other employers. The employers may have been unable to combine with the weavers to support the list, nevertheless no one had a greater interest in seeing that one manufacturer paid according to the list of prices than another manufacturer engaged in the same trade, and from time to time the masters in one branch of the trade may even have contributed to the support of the weavers on strike against the masters in another.[3]

On many occasions the weavers' tactics were sufficient to restore the trade to order. When the disputes became more general, however, the weavers had to set about the matter in another way, by appealing to the conscience of the whole town. They canvassed 'the more respectable inhabitants of the city', obtaining their signatures to a requisition to the Mayor to call a town meeting, to 'resolve the unhappy differences between masters and men'.[4] In the 1830's, many of the honourable manufacturers still signed these requisitions and attended the meetings. But the greater part of the fifty or sixty signatures on many of the requisitions were those of shopkeepers,[5] members of

---

[1] e.g. the *Coventry Herald*, 2 October 1829, 29 August 1834, and the *Coventry Standard*, 31 July 1840.

[2] e.g. the *Coventry Standard*, 31 March 1843.   [3] ibid, 9 June 1848.

[4] e.g. the *Coventry Herald*, 6 February 1835, the *Coventry Standard*, 31 July 1840. *Reports Commissioners, 1840*, XXIV, pp. 227-8.

[5] The shopkeepers sometimes gave credit to the weavers when they were on strike, *Reports Commissioners, 1840*, XXIV, p. 234.

the professions, and gentlemen (i.e. men of no occupation and a fixed address).

It is not easy to describe what followed without seeming to burlesque, but the upshot usually was that the Mayor presided over the meeting, the weavers presented their case, nobody appeared to answer it, and the meeting appointed a committee of the respectable inhabitants to go the round of the offending manufacturers politely asking them to start paying by the list of prices again.[1] At this point the manufacturers protested one after another to the committee that each of them was willing, personally, to pay according to the list, provided his competitors would do the same. One or two stopped to lay the blame on the weavers for taking out the work below list prices. Hardly any, at this time, dared to fly in the face of public opinion and denounce the list as such. In this way things were generally patched up after two or three weeks' disturbance—until the next time.

These events happened almost every year, and sometimes more than once in the year, and it would be wearisome and pointless to reiterate the history of the successive disputes in detail. The critical point was that the weavers should keep the public opinion of the town on their side, and they knew that to do this they must not use violence or damage property. The members of the committee of the weavers' union invariably warned their followers against the use of force. In 1829, the weavers at their meeting resolved not to use 'irritable language', even to those who had reduced wages.[2] As one of the committee, Mr. Goode, put it,

at present all the respectable inhabitants of Coventry are our friends: the manufacturers, the Magistracy, and all the influential of the inhabitants: take care, therefore, that we don't make them our enemies.[3]

In this period restraint and dignity were, indeed, often shown on both sides.

Nevertheless, the decision not to use force did not rule out a demonstration of unity and strength, and the weavers who were on strike were accustomed to parade the streets of the town, with

[1] *Reports Commissioners, 1840*, XXIV, pp. 248-9.
[2] The *Coventry Herald*, 13 March 1829.   [3] ibid, 8 May 1829.

or without banners and bands, before squatting down on Greyfriars Green to hear the latest news of the negotiations from the members of their committee. From time to time, of course, these demonstrations got out of hand. The Magistrates did not mind the weavers burning one of their employers in effigy,[1] but they tended to draw the line at the production of a donkey for parading the offending master round the streets—tended to, because in 1819 they had apparently winked at such a proceeding.[2] But by 1831 there is no doubt that the Magistrates would have defended Mr. Beck had they been able. A body of determined weavers, however, could still brush the constables aside, and from time to time, as in 1829, the Mayor had to go to meet the weavers in person, with the other Magistrates, and to assure them that they could have his good offices if they would only be orderly.[3]

Despite the unfortunate destruction of Mr. Beck's factory in 1831, the weavers' tactics, and the warm sympathy of the better class of masters and of the town in general, evidently resulted in the years 1830 to 1833 being marked by a general return to the principles of the list of prices.[4] The weavers kept their organization intact, and the better class of masters at last managed to form one of their own. Only sixteen manufacturers attended the first meeting in May 1830,[5] but in November of the next year no fewer than seventy-two of the manufacturers actually met to agree on a list of prices for the single hand trade, which had probably never had one since the introduction of the Dutch engine loom.[6] In 1832 the Ribbon Manufacturers' Association established a committee of twenty to negotiate with the weavers' committee, and several outstanding technical issues were settled between them.[7] In November 1833 the manufacturers' association unanimously resolved that,

---

[1] The *Coventry Herald*, 15 May 1829.

[2] George Hall, *Prize Essay*, 1861, p. 13, and *Reports Commissioners, 1835*, XXV, p. 426.

[3] The *Coventry Herald*, 2 October 1829.

[4] The connexion between the destruction of Mr. Beck's factory and the current labour disputes is partly elucidated in *Reports Commissioners, 1840*, XXIV, pp. 236-7.

[5] The *Coventry Herald*, 28 May 1830.

[6] ibid, 11 November 1831, and *Reports Commissioners, 1840*, XXIV, pp. 238-9.

[7] The *Coventry Herald*, 13 January 1832, and 16 November 1832.

whenever a difficulty occurs manufacturers should at all times be ready to meet to remove it,

because the alternative would be to destroy the harmony of the last two years.[1] But, at this point, the manufacturers' association apparently dissolved into thin air. From 1834 onwards it would be left to the united weavers, to individual masters, and to the public opinion of the town to maintain the list of prices if they could.

The years 1830-33 seem to have been the Indian summer of the old system of industrial relations in Coventry. For the last time the good masters and the good men had won a complete victory over the bad masters and the bad men, while public opinion approved of their victory. The majority, who were good, had been greatly helped in their struggle by the attitude of the press, for both the *Standard*'s predecessor, the *Mercury*, and the *Herald*, were at this time in favour of the list. The power of the local journalists was not confined to writing editorials. Much the most valuable thing the local papers could do was to report the meetings of the weavers verbatim, and if the weavers said that somebody was a bad man, to print their words without comment. The names of both masters and men were printed in the newspapers. In 1829 the *Herald* gave an account of a weavers' meeting at which it was announced that some workmen were taking out work at reduced prices.

'Name? name?' from all parts of the room. At length two persons names were announced: 'Pollard of Much Park Street', and 'Thomas of Spon Street'. The cry became general in the room, 'then let's go in a body to their houses.'[2]

The ordinary weaver obviously had more to lose from a visitation by his fellow workmen who were convinced he was a blackleg, than from the publication of his name in the press: not so the manufacturer, to whom publicity of this kind must generally have been distasteful. George Eliot's Mr. Vincy, for instance, liked to entertain,[3] and we are given to believe that people would soon have found excuses for avoiding his dinner

---

[1] The *Coventry Herald*, 15 November 1833, and *Reports Commissioners, 1840*, XXIV, pp. 241-2.

[2] The *Coventry Herald*, 8 May 1829.

[3] George Eliot, *Middlemarch*, World's Classics, 1947, pp. 243, 368.

parties had they seen reports in the newspapers to the effect that he was dishonourable.

The *Standard* regularly published the names of the manufacturers with whom the weavers were in dispute, together with the comments of the men upon them, until the trade collapsed in the sixties. The *Herald* was not quite so free with names, but there were two Charles Brays in the ribbon trade, and it must have pleased the Charles Bray of Rosehill and Much Park Street, (who owned the *Herald*), to print the following:

Mr. Haymes hoped that he would not be misunderstood when he referred to Mr. Charles Bray. He would observe that two men of one name, sustaining such opposite characters, could not be found in any other town in England than that of Mr. Charles Bray of Much Park Street, and that of Mr. Charles Bray of Earl Street. The latter was the drag weight that hangs like a millstone round our necks, preventing our social progress; the other had the honour and gratitude of the working men of Coventry . . . a more honourable master did not exist. He had known him, when a man took out a new pattern and agreed to the price, . . . to say to his warehouseman, 'I think we can give a little more for this; let the man have a little profit as well as ourselves.'[1]

This extract shows, incidentally, why Mr. Charles Bray of Much Park Street did not make a success of business. But it is important because it shows the freedom with which the newspapers reported the words of the weavers about their masters. As soon as the new generation of Mr. Charles Brays of Earl Street, who did not care what the weavers said or the newspapers published about them, took control of the trade the list of prices would be in real danger.

Many of these small masters already adhered to, even if they did not yet openly avow, the arguments against the payment of wages according to agreed lists of prices which were now to be heard all over England, and which were even at this very time resulting in the abandonment of the list among the carpet weavers of Kidderminster.[2] These were based upon the assumptions that any agreement to fix wages in this way was a conspiracy against the consumer and the community as a whole, and an infringement of the Englishman's right to do what he

---

[1] The *Coventry Herald*, 15 March 1850.   [2] ibid, 27 June 1828.

liked with his own—i.e. to sell his labour for what it would fetch.[1]

The weavers of Coventry admitted that there might be some truth in the first contention, but countered it with the argument that the consumption of ribbons was regulated by fashion rather than by price, and that even if the list were abandoned and ribbons became cheaper, the number of ribbons bought and sold would remain exactly the same. In these circumstances they did not see why they should not continue to receive the living wage to which they were accustomed.

The second criticism of the list was met by the argument that the freedom of the labourer to sell his labour was in no way infringed by the labourers combining to sell their labour at a fair price. Furthermore, the weavers argued, the freedom of the manufacturers was as great with a list of prices as it was without one. At all times the manufacturers were free to employ good workmen before bad ones, and the fact that every manufacturer had to pay the same price for labour ensured that the competition between one manufacturer and another was fair.

The weavers knew that without a list, competition among the unscrupulous masters, taking advantage of the needs of the men, would lead to a reduction of wages all round. The good weavers would then be paid the same low wages that the bad weavers would earn on a free market. This was why the weavers of Coventry were prepared to defend the list of prices even if they had to starve to do it. On this one point they were blind to argument. The alternative to the list was free labour: under either system the good workman and the bad workman were going to be paid much the same as each other. It was better, surely, in that case, for both of them to be paid a decent living wage, than for both of them to be starved slowly, like the country weavers, on a low one?

[1] The arguments can be found *in extenso* in *Reports Committees, 1818*, IX, when the possibility of extending the Spitalfields Act to Coventry was considered. These arguments are condensed in *Reports Commissioners, 1840*, XXIV, pp. 217-30. There is a useful summary of the weavers' arguments in favour of the list of prices in the *Coventry Standard*, 20 July 1860.

IV

THE WAGES AND STANDARDS OF LIVING OF THE DIFFERENT CLASSES OF RIBBON WEAVERS

IN the country villages to the north and north-east of Coventry, where the weavers had no list of prices and competed with their single hand looms against the more advanced looms of the city, the wages were low. Where both the father and the mother were weaving, the whole family was wretched, with no hope of improvement save by becoming undertakers, and subjecting others to the state from which they had just risen.[1] A majority of the fathers, however, were colliers or quarrymen,[2] and rough as life was in the area between Coventry and Nuneaton, always boisterous and sometimes barbarous, it was nothing like so bad as the pitiful life of the Manchester cellars.

In fact, three-quarters of the country weavers were said to be women, and seven-eighths women and children.[3] The children were set to work at eight to ten years of age. No child earned more than one shilling and sixpence a week, and these miserable wages, paid to their parents, were still sufficient, so low had the district sunk, to cause their fathers and mothers to bring them to the labour market.[4] Wages in this instance, as the Assistant Commissioner to the Unemployed Handloom Weavers Commission pointed out, had as demoralizing an influence on the working class as poor relief.[5] At these wages the children were expected to work from 7 a.m. to 8 p.m.,[6] but like their elders, they presumably did very little work on Mondays and finished work early on Saturdays.

At any age from ten to fourteen the little winders of both sexes were put into the loom.[7] They would not be apprenticed, though there seems to have been a custom for some sort of rough and ready indenture to be drawn up, which would not

---

[1] *Reports Commissioners, 1840*, XXIV, p. 55. [2] ibid, p. 54. [3] ibid, p. 54.
[4] ibid, p. 53. [5] ibid, p. 322. [6] ibid, p. 53. [7] ibid, p. 53.

have been binding at law.[1] Other girls were taken into the trade
at fourteen or fifteen, their parents being paid three to four
shillings a week, and the masters hiring them each year, by the
year, at a slightly increased rate, until at sixteen or seventeen
they qualified as journeymen, and received their own wages.[2]
In the country districts it was still the custom to pay the
journeymen two-thirds of the price paid by the manufacturer to
the undertaker. In the 1830's this would have amounted to
about five shillings a week when the trade was busy, and over
the course of the year must have averaged less.[3] Such a wage
might be a useful addition to the earnings of a collier's family,
but it was disastrously low for the few men remaining in the
weaving trade. For this wage the custom was, as in the city, to
work over sixty hours a week.[4] Monday would be a holiday,
while the remainder of the last week's wages was being spent,
and possibly part of Tuesday too. To make up for this the
weavers worked longer and longer hours as the week went by,
sometimes staying up much of Friday night in order to finish
their pieces in time for the undertaker to carry them to the
manufacturer's warehouse on the Saturday afternoon.[5]

In the city and in Foleshill it was common for the children
to attend dame or charity school for a year or two before
starting work at about nine or ten years of age.[6] A few months
after they had started work many of the boys were apprenticed,
their indentures being properly drawn up and signed on behalf
of the boy's father, the boy's master, and the city whose
freedom was the prize.[7] There were on an average about 100
boys apprenticed to the weaving trade every year in the 1830's,
and the custom of apprenticeship seems to have been very
little affected by the Reform Act of 1832.[8] There was almost
certainly an attraction about serving an apprenticeship, a
belief that a good workman ought to serve one, in addition to
the desire to make certain of a parliamentary vote. Yet another
reason for the survival of this custom was that it was advantage-
ous to all the families concerned. Respectable families became

---

[1] *Reports Commissioners, 1840*, XXIV, p. 54.   [2] ibid, pp. 54-55.

[3] ibid, p. 53.   [4] ibid, p. 299.   [5] ibid, pp. 91-92.

[6] Education is discussed at length in *Reports Commissioners, 1840*, XXIV,
Section III.

[7] ibid, p. 61.

[8] See the Register of Apprentices' Indentures in the City Record Office.

connected through apprenticeships, and the apprentice helped
the ordinary first-hand journeyman, or outdoor weaver,
through the difficult period of his life when he was paying
heavily for his own children while they were still too young to
work.[1]

Wages were paid in the city by the piece according to the
list of prices.[2] The prices paid to the first-hand journeymen and
to the factory operatives seem to have been much the same,
except that a shilling or so was taken from the factory operative's
wage on account of the 'loom and room', i.e. the fixed capital
that the first-hand journeyman had to find for himself. This
was probably fair, for the first-hand journeyman generally
found that he had to pay out about the same sum in repairs to
his loom, and he had in addition to pay the rent of his weaver's
shop. Working at the Dutch engine loom, the first-hand
journeyman might expect to make ten shillings and sixpence a
week, and the factory hand nine shillings and sixpence. In the
Jacquard trade, the first-hand journeyman working on his own
account could average fifteen shillings and sixpence, the first-
hand journeyman working for a manufacturer could make
fourteen shillings, and the factory hand thirteen shillings. This,
however, was in the highest paying factories in Coventry. In
Bedworth the Jacquard factory hand only received from nine
shillings to twelve shillings, and in Nuneaton the wages were
eight to nine shillings only.

The journeymen's journeymen worked either in the factories,
at factory prices, or for the first-hand journeymen, in which
case they usually received the manufacturer's price less two
shillings or two shillings and threepence retained by the first-
hands as loom and room rent and profit. The journeymen's
journeymen, therefore, used to make about eight shillings or
eight shillings and sixpence a week in the plain-engine trade,
and in the Jacquard trade, where the deductions for expenses
tended to be higher, about ten shillings and sixpence.

The winders' and warpers' earnings varied a lot, from five
shillings to eleven shillings a week for winders, with an average

---

[1] *Reports Commissioners, 1840,* XXIV, p. 76.

[2] One manufacturer, Mr. Day, seems to have paid by the week. The details are
from *Reports Commissioners, 1840,* XXIV, Chapter VI, especially the Tables on
pp. 304-5.

of perhaps six shillings or six shillings and sixpence, and from eight shillings to eighteen shillings, with an average of ten shillings for warpers. All these figures are deceptive, however, unless one remembers to think in terms of families instead of individuals. The family with one wage earner was the exception while many families had three or four.

The factory hands had more regular habits than the outdoor weavers, but at this time the factory hands, like the outdoor weavers, seem to have done very little work on Mondays, not starting until after breakfast, and leaving off in the middle of the afternoon at 'Club time'. Both classes probably worked longer hours, if they were in work, in the summer. Mrs. Dresser, a factory owner, said in 1838 that her employees worked twelve hours in summer and ten and a half in winter. The men said they worked twelve hours.[1]

The outdoor weavers were free to choose their hours of work, and the Coventry weavers do not seem to have adopted the very effective method of limiting the hours of work of their neighbours, which was practised at this time in St. Etienne. There the weavers threw stones through the windows of any workshop where lights were seen burning after the agreed hours.[2] The weavers' houses of Coventry, with their long windows would have made easy targets. The freedom to work in your own time seems to have been one of the greatest attractions of working at home. As the brickmakers and colliers of the country districts put it,

it was very hard on them to be turned out at early hours every day, instead of being able to take what hours they please, like the ribbon weaver: and, like him, take *Saint* Monday, and *Saint* Tuesday too, if they choose.[3]

The details of wages and hours of work are of little help in assessing the standard of living of the weavers, until one can say for how much of the year the weaver might reasonably expect to be employed. Unemployment had always followed the seasonal variations in the trade, but was now believed to be more closely

---

[1] *Reports Commissioners, 1840,* XXIV, p. 298.

[2] Public Record Office, Home Office Papers, O.S. 6967, Letter from Robert Baker, H.M. Factory Inspector, to Sir George Lewis, enclosing the reports of the delegations sent from Coventry to France in 1860.

[3] *Reports Commissioners, 1840,* XXIV, p. 94.

tied to the trade cycle.[1] Whereas, early in the century, one could
have said with some confidence that the average weaver might
expect to lose two months in the year during the summer, by
the thirties he was apparently just as likely to be out of work for
two months one year and not at all the next. Much the same
considerations apply to any attempt to assess the time lost
through industrial disputes. These mostly occurred when many
people were out of work and both masters and men were
tempted to break the list. One branch of the trade, or the hands
working for one master, might strike work for three or four
weeks in one year, and then not strike again for several years.
Some classes of weavers, like the journeymen's journeymen,
working for the first-hands, probably never had strikes at all. If
one were able to take an average, it might show, perhaps, that
in the 1830's the ordinary weaver lost six weeks in the year from
the slackness of trade, and a few days only through strikes.

Any attempt to present the weavers' standard of living
statistically is further complicated by the fact that the different
classes of weaver were not laid off at the same time. First to go
were the country weavers, on the margin, while a manufacturer
who was engaged in both the factory and the outdoor trade,
naturally laid off his outdoor hands before dismissing his factory
ones. Everyone tried to throw the losses of bad trade on to somebody else. The twenty-seven factory owners of 1838 had 598
looms in their factories, and employed a further 1,264 looms
outside.[2] The factory owner's ideal was obviously to have fixed
capital, in buildings and looms, only to the amount that he
could be sure to employ all the year round, and for the rest, to
employ outdoor weavers who rented their own houses and
owned their own looms. The outdoor weavers working for
manufacturers with factories could thus be compelled to carry
much of the burden of fixed capital standing idle during a
recession. This was undoubtedly a serious handicap to the
first-hand journeymen in their long struggle with the factory
operatives, whom they looked down on as an inferior class.

When he was out of work, the weaver might, like Gutteridge
and many other freemen, refuse to go on the parish, and starve,
or he might accept relief.[3] The choice the weaver made may

---

[1] *Reports Commissioners, 1840*, XXIV, p. 70.   [2] ibid, Table X, p. 63.
[3] See above, p. 14, and the *Coventry Standard*, 14 April 1837.

also be said to have affected his standard of living. Poor relief may not be as good for one's self-respect as starvation, but it is a great deal better for one's health. Strictly speaking, if there is something to be subtracted from the weaver's standard of living for the time he spent unemployed, there is also something to be added for the amount he received in poor relief. The total expenditure on relief in Coventry in the united parishes of St. Michael's and Holy Trinity fell from a yearly average of approximately £14,000 in the 1820's and 1830's, to an average of less than £10,000 in the 1840's and about £7,000 in the 1850's.[1] At the same time the population had nearly doubled. This money was mostly levied from about 2,000 of the richer inhabitants and mostly paid to about 2,000 of the older and poorer ones,[2] and while some weavers may have received the equivalent of several weeks' wages every year from this source, others never received anything at all.

The freeman who did not care to take relief from the parish might yet be willing to benefit from the charitable funds established under the patronage of the Mayor, the clergy, and the gentlemen of the town during periods of extreme distress. Apart from the cholera funds of 1832 and 1849, relief funds were set up during periods of depressed trade in 1823 and 1837, in the spring and again in the winter in 1841, in 1847 and 1855, and again in rather different circumstances in 1860. The procedure followed on these occasions was as stereotyped as that followed by the weavers when they were trying to resist attempts to break the list of prices.[3] A number of respectable inhabitants signed a requisition to the Mayor to call a town meeting, the Mayor agreed, and the meeting was held in St. Mary's Hall. The Mayor presided, the clergy reminded the audience of the high authority on which they knew that the poor must always be with them, and of the sacred duty of Christian charity, the manufacturers testified to the fortitude with which the weavers were bearing their misfortune, and everyone agreed that the money given would not be wasted. The richer inhabitants generally responded with contributions totalling £700 or £800,

---

[1] The Accounts were published in the *Coventry Herald* and the *Coventry Standard*.

[2] See the Burgess lists, and the Overseers' Accounts.

[3] e.g. the *Coventry Standard* and the *Coventry Herald*, 29 January 1841, and 19 March 1841.

which were invariably used to buy bread, and a committee, which included several weavers acquainted with the worst cases of distress, arranged the distribution of the loaves. In this way hundreds or even thousands of families received one 4 lb. loaf a week while the depression lasted. It was better than nothing, but it was not inspiring fare.

In the 1830's the 4 lb. loaf generally cost about 6*d*. or 7*d*., butter 1*s*. 6*d*. a lb., cheese 7*d*. or 8*d*., a lb., cheap tea 4*s*. a lb., and potatoes 3*s*. a cwt. Bacon sometimes cost as little as 2*d*. or 3*d*. a lb.[1] In the following decade prices, on the whole, tended to come down, and the forties were not especially 'hungry' in Coventry. A number of imported foods became available at reasonable prices, and in 1842 H. Simons advertised that thanks to Sir Robert Peel's budget he could now offer corned beef from New York at 2¾*d*. to 4*d*. a lb., and prime rounds of beef from Russia at 4½*d*. a lb.[2] At the same time other commodities in everyday use, like soap and candles, cost about 7*d*. or 8*d*. a lb. each, while coal cost as little as 7*d*. or 8*d*. a cwt.[3] Thus a hundredweight of coal cost about as much in those days as a pound of candles, while potatoes cost about five times as much as coal. At these prices it is easy to see that in a family with only one wage earner, there would not be much left over, after the weekly housekeeping, for clothes, or house rent, or furniture, let alone for that great objective of so many weavers' savings, a loom. An engine loom cost £40, a Jacquard even more,[4] and a weaver, if he was to save enough money to buy a loom, must do it before he married.

With these prices in mind it is not astonishing to find that all the country weavers had to live on was bread, potatoes, and a little tea, and sometimes a few poor scraps of bacon. Milk, at a penny a quart or so, must have been within their reach, and at Exhall at any rate, many of them had gardens of their own, though elsewhere the letting of potato ground, or allotments, by the farmers was not common.[5]

The cottages in the country districts were, of course, a

---

[1] *Reports Commissioners, 1840*, XXIV, pp. 310-11.
[2] The *Coventry Herald*, 21 October 1842.
[3] *Reports Commissioners, 1840*, XXIV, pp. 310-11.
[4] Joseph Gutteridge, *Lights and Shadows*, &c., 1893, p. 149.
[5] *Reports Commissioners, 1840*, XXIV, p. 318.

disgrace. Looking at them from the road, one beheld behind the windows

a pale, sickly looking man or woman pressing a narrow chest against a board, and doing a sort of treadmill work with legs and arms.[1]

Inside, scattered round the weaver, there might be a stool, an old table, and a chair. In one corner lay the bed, made of straw if the family was 'well off', and of chaff if it was not. The bedstead would have been made of bricks.[2]

The girls naturally all 'kept company', and were pregnant before they married at sixteen or seventeen. Bastardy was common, and no censure attached to it in that society, whatever the Parliament at Westminster or their 'betters' might think.[3] The girls, being brought up from an early age to the weaving, knew nothing of domestic economy, and there were few large houses in the district where they could go into domestic service and learn how to keep house. In any case, the men scorned to marry servant girls, preferring the weavers for their wages.[4] Their wives being unable to make them decent homes, the men passed their evenings in the gin shops, where they spent their own and their wives' wages.

This was the weaving area at its worst. The weavers were treated, as C. R. Fay has pointed out, like marginal land in the theories of the classical economists, the area of cultivation expanding and contracting according to the demand.[5] Occasional cultivation of this kind is bad, as Fay says, for people as well as land. There were few middle class people left in that district to set a better standard, or to provide a kind of public opinion to which the weavers could appeal for just treatment and fair wages.[6] It would have been difficult, as one observer said, to have imagined a darker picture:

the single-hand trade of the country not only exhibits the greatest demoralisation at home, but helps to fill the criminal calendars of neighbouring counties.[7]

[1] George Eliot, *Scenes of Clerical Life*, 'The Sad Fortunes of the Rev. Amos Barton'. Chapter II.

[2] *Reports Commissioners, 1840*, XXIV, pp. 93, 318.   [3] ibid, pp. 94-95.

[4] ibid, p. 96.

[5] C. R. Fay, *Life and Labour in the Nineteenth Century*, Cambridge University Press, 1920, p. 176.

[6] *Reports Commissioners, 1840*, XXIV, p. 250.   [7] ibid, p. 97.

There was no rural innocence and happiness to the north of Coventry. To the south of the city among the purely agricultural villages it seems to have been different, with many good cottages, low rents, tidy gardens, and well-clothed children. In the city too, things were very much better. There the tone was set by the first-hand journeymen—that superior class of (mostly) freemen weavers working at home. Their wages were not as high, it is true, as those of the skilled workers in other trades. In 1838 the carpenter in Coventry received about 23s. a week, the mason 21s., and a watchmaker anything from 18s. to 30s. according to his skill.[1] But the first-hand journeymen of Coventry were much better off than the broad silk weavers in Spitalfields and Macclesfield, and the Assistant Commissioner to the Unemployed Handloom Weavers Commission experienced the liveliest gratification at seeing the superiority of habits of the Coventry weavers.[2]

The first-hand journeymen fed much better than the country weavers, for even if one loom only brought in ten shillings a week, most of them had two looms or more. Their wives had kitchen ranges on which to cook, and in prosperous times they had been known to patronize the poultry market.[3] Even in normal times, however, they earned enough to have puddings and cakes, in addition to the staple foods of porridge, potatoes, bread and butter, and milk. They may sometimes have had a little sugar with their tea. Supper, with beer, was their main meal of the day, and on Sundays they had a little meat for dinner in the middle of the day.[4] Their wives, in fact, could generally manage pretty well. The men were not driven out of their homes by the discomfort, but, in the evenings, in order to be sociable and to relax, they enjoyed spending 5d. on a couple of glasses of ale and a pipe in the smoking-room of a public house.[5]

The public house, indeed, sometimes played quite a large part in their lives, for in Coventry as in other towns, there were yards where the public house owned the only water tap, and where in return for the use of the tap you were expected from time to time to buy a little ale too.[6] More important still

---

[1] *Reports Commissioners, 1840*, XXIV, pp. 306-7.   [2] ibid, p. 89.
[3] ibid, p. 89.   [4] ibid, p. 317.   [5] ibid, p. 89.
[6] Verbal communication from Mr. Walter Dunn.

to most of these first-hands was the fact that some of the public houses organized benefit clubs. Monday evening was known throughout the city as 'Club time', and it was then that the weaver with a little money to lay aside put it into the local (public house) provident society, rather than into the newly opened savings bank, where, in 1838, there were no more than 100 weaver depositors.[1] In 1851 thirty-two of the 202 public houses in the city organized fifty-six clubs between them, with 2,930 members.[2] The weaver did not put money into the savings bank for fear that the employer would come to hear of it, and make it an excuse to reduce his wages. The savings bank was part of 'them': the public house on the other hand was part of 'us', and there was no fear that the landlord would disclose his accounts to the manufacturers.

In 1851 fifty out of the fifty-six public house provident societies were sickness clubs. Consequently they were greatly concerned about the merits of doctors. Let it not be supposed, says George Eliot, that opinion at the Tankard in Slaughter Lane was unimportant to the medical profession:

that old authentic public house—the original Tankard, known by the name of Dollop's—was the resort of a great Benefit Club, which had some months before put to the vote whether its long standing medical man, 'Doctor Gambit', should not be cashiered in favour of 'this Doctor Lydgate', who was capable of performing the most astonishing cures, and rescuing people altogether given up by other practitioners.[3]

The houses of this class of weaver cost from £8 to £10 a year.[4] There was a choice of two story and three story houses, with three or four rooms and a workshop. Typical of the two story houses, which formed a large part of the development of Hillfields in the 1830's, was 20 Castle Street (see figure 4). The front door opened straight into the parlour, but then was the front door ever used? Entering the house, instead, from the back, via the entry and the scullery, one came to the comfortable kitchen, with its corner range. From there, a staircase led upstairs to the big room at the back of the house, which

---

[1] *Reports Commissioners, 1840*, XXIV, pp. 89-90.
[2] The *Coventry Herald*, 1 August 1851.
[3] George Eliot, *Middlemarch*, World's Classics, 1947, p. 472.
[4] *Reports Commissioners, 1840*, XXIV, p. 294.

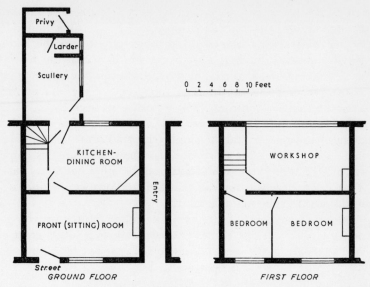

FIG. 4. 20 Castle Street, Hillfields: a two story weaver's house.

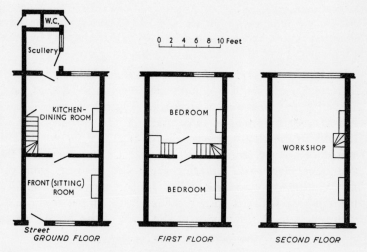

FIG. 5. 11 Vernon Street, Hillfields: a three story weaver's house.

PLATE 2.

Two and three story weavers' houses in Brook Street, Hillfields.

was used as a workshop, and to the two bedrooms in the front of the house.

The three story houses were better arranged (see figure 5). They were narrow, with the top story given up entirely to the 'topshop', or weaving loft, where there was room for two or three looms. With windows on both sides of the topshop there was generally an even light to work by. To insulate the rest of the house from the noise of the weaving, rags were commonly stuffed between the floor of the topshop and the ceilings of the bedrooms below.[1] Outside the city, in Hillfields, both the two story and the three story houses normally had small but valuable gardens. Many of these houses of the first-hand journeymen were well furnished, with a clock downstairs, good beds and chests of drawers upstairs, and prints on the parlour walls.[2]

This was the standard of living of the first-hand journeymen at a time when trade was good. The journeymen's journeymen, working either for the first-hands, or in the factories, must have enjoyed a slightly lower standard of living commensurate with their lower wages, though some of them were no doubt able, since they were less provident and less inclined to save, to spend money as freely as the first-hands. Many of these journeymen's journeymen, and the factory hands below them, were, however, still living in the smaller, cramped houses of the old city, with two rooms and no garden. There is no need to attempt a separate assessment of their standard of living, for the condition of all these classes may be measured by the good old nineteenth century yardstick. If an artisan could afford no bacon, he was badly off. If he could afford bacon, but no meat, then he was doing middling well. If he could afford butcher's meat, and had a clock in the house, then he was very well off indeed. In the first category one can place the country weavers, in the second the factory hands and the journeymen's journeymen, and in the third the first-hand journeymen.

Silk weaving was not always a healthy occupation. The windows of a weaver's shop would normally have had to be kept closed. The silk was handed out and returned by weight, and contact with the open air changed the moisture content and the

---

[1] Verbal communication from Mr. Walter Dunn.
[2] *Reports Commissioners, 1840*, XXIV, p. 317.

weight of the silk. Smoke was damaging, and the ordinary weaver had to work all through the winter without a fire. The weaver's position at the loom was cramped, with his breast resting against it.[1] This, and the early age at which the weavers were put into the loom, was considered to account for the characteristically small stature and for the stoop of the weavers, for the small development of many of their muscles, and for their pale countenances. Although many weavers seem to have gone to the Peninsula,[2] they were not as a rule reckoned good material for the recruiting sergeant.

The dyer and the collier were accounted larger than the weaver, but the weavers were believed to be more intelligent:

the difference between them and a body of navigators was seen most conspicuously in a mob fight at an election not long ago. The navigators expected to fight a pitched battle with fists, but the weavers broke their ranks, closed in upon them, and completely beat them by numbers.[3]

Men of this kind probably suffered less from physical ailments than from the mental strain occasioned by the fear of unemployment, and by the fear of old age. The country weavers were, perhaps, so degraded that it meant nothing to them whether they or their neighbours were laid off, and whether they died in their own beds or in the workhouse. But to the average factory hand and journeyman's journeyman in the city these were constant worries, while to the best class of weavers, the first-hands, they must have been a nightmare, for the first-hands, with their good wages and provident ways, had given many hostages to fortune.[4]

The happiness of the weavers might depend also upon their being within reach of the countryside, and upon their having sports and pastimes. Many of the people in the centre of the city had no gardens, but none of them was at this time far away from the Lammas and Michaelmas lands. In the new red brick suburb of Hillfields, with its new red brick church, St. Peter's, there were both gardens and the open countryside. Gutteridge, recalling the appearance of Primrose Hill, said that at this time,

it well deserved the name it bore, for in my early recollection it was a

---

[1] *Reports Commissioners, 1840*, XXIV, p. 317.

[2] ibid, p. 50.   [3] ibid, p. 316.   [4] ibid, p. 317.

mass of primroses and daffodils, while the lower and damper parts were yellow with the flowers of the lesser pilewort.[1]

Like other boys at all times Gutteridge had gone climbing elm trees to steal crow's eggs, and fishing in the streams round the city. As the city expanded these recreations became more remote. In 1893 Gutteridge complained that the birds which were common in his youth no longer came into the city.

The woodlark seems all but extinct in this locality, as does also the goldfinch: the brown linnet and the golden crested wren are scarce. In fact, many of the small birds, both stationary and migratory have disappeared, and we have now to travel some miles from the town before we can see . . . [them].[2]

The only possible conclusion is that in the 1830's if one was interested in nature, one could find it. Serious study would have been beyond most, but pleasurable appreciation was there for anyone. In this respect at least, life in Coventry was what you cared to make it. There were roses round the door of the cottage in which Gutteridge met his fiancée, and she and her mother were poor enough.[3]

Music was a favourite recreation in Gutteridge's family, and he well remembered how his taste was fostered by the concerts given by his father and uncles, all of whom had been in their regimental bands during the Napoleonic wars.[4] Nobody in Coventry, whether he had musical relations or not, need ever have gone wholly tuneless, with the lovely bells of St. Michael's raised high over the centre of the city. Bray used to listen to them at Rosehill, just outside the city,[5] and every working man on every side must have been accustomed to listen for them as they struck the hours of work away. Nowadays everyone wears a watch, and the city has spread too far, and the traffic is too noisy, for the bells to make the same impression. The weavers who listened to the bells did not, however, mostly go to church or chapel. In 1851, when 'the religious census' was taken one Sunday morning, there were only 2,917 people at the churches of the city, and 2,963 at the chapels. This means that only about one person in six attended Sunday worship.[6]

[1] Joseph Gutteridge, *Lights and Shadows*, &c., 1893, p. 20.   [2] ibid, p. 16.
[3] ibid, p. 42.   [4] ibid, p. 12.
[5] Charles Bray, *Phases of Opinion*, &c., 1884, pp. 69-70.
[6] The *Coventry Herald*, 1 August 1851.

There were no regular holidays except at Christmas, and on Good Friday (which was not then a working day), and Easter, unless you took 'Saint' Monday. As the time when he had most leisure, which was when he was out of work, was also the time when he had least money, the ordinary weaver probably only left Coventry once or twice in his life. The experiences of William Andrews, who grew tired of looking for work, and set off on a tour round the south of England, or went to Switzerland, were exceptional. Even by modern standards Andrews would have been accounted a well-travelled man. Most people took their recreation at home, in the city, at the annual Godiva procession, and at the parliamentary elections that took place every few years. The old, rough street sports of bull and duck baiting were dying out, and giving place to bowls and skittles.[1] But there was always gambling at the Green Dragon,[2] though, as George Eliot says, there was better gambling at billiards or anything else, at Brassing (Birmingham).[3]

[1] *Reports Commissioners, 1840,* XXIV, p. 315.
[2] George Eliot, *Middlemarch,* World's Classics, 1947, p. 726.   [3] ibid, p. 719.

V

THE TRANSFORMATION OF THE RIBBON TRADE IN THE 1840's AND 1850's

GENERAL FEATURES OF THE TRANSFORMATION

IN 1830 the old structure of industry survived, there was no class war, and a majority of the masters and of the workmen employed in the ribbon trade agreed that it was in the interests of the community to maintain the list of prices, and the standards of life which the list guaranteed. The rest of the community so far agreed with them that the public opinion of the town, working through the Magistrates and the shopkeepers, actively assisted this majority of honourable masters and men in their attempts to impose the accepted standards upon the whole trade. There had always been cracks in this structure, for every master and every workman was at one time or another tempted to break the list, and for the next thirty years these cracks widened, until the whole structure collapsed in 1860, and the list of prices was abandoned.

In the first place, the old masters, who were still ready to combine in support of the list in the early 1830's, continued to give way steadily both in the trade and in the town before the new, small masters. At first these new masters, true to their creed, would combine with nobody and compete with everybody, but in 1860 they too were ready to combine, together with the remaining old masters whom they had brought down to their own level to overthrow the list.

In the second place, the city weavers, who had always been divided from the country weavers, were themselves becoming divided into two classes, for the intermediate class of journeymen's journeymen no longer bridged the gap between the first-hands and the factory operatives. As the factories became more efficient, and the factory owners could afford to pay higher, weekly wages, the factory operatives became less dependent upon the list of prices for their standard of living, while the outdoor weavers, whose techniques were less efficient, became more dependent upon the list than ever. The list had always been a protection for the weavers working at the less advanced looms. By the 1850's the class working the less advanced looms, the first-hands, was also the class accustomed to the highest standard of living. The differences of interest between the two classes, which became all the more apparent because the factories were concentrated in the old town and the outdoor weavers in the suburb of Hillfields, could not be concealed for ever by the single trade union which, from 1856 onwards, represented the workers in both branches of the trade.

In the third place the public opinion which had supported the praiseworthy attempt to pay just wages dissolved. The old fashioned Tory Mayors and Magistrates gave way to Liberal ones, who mixed half understood principles of political economy with the administration of justice. The shopkeepers' sympathy was alienated by the way in which the outdoor weavers, who controlled the weavers' union, intimidated the factory operatives into striking work at a time when they could have been earning good wages and spending their money in the shops. Finally, the new manufacturers were less sensitive to what was said about them. This can be attributed partly to the growth of the city. The person, who, in a society of 1,000 people, has 200 acquaintances, will generally in a society of 2,000 continue to have the same number. In the latter case, however, they will be much less likely to concern themselves with each other's conduct in business. Certainly the population of Coventry doubled between 1821 and 1861. Nothing could be more human than an increase in the population, and nothing could be further from the control of any single human being. It is a point that would have delighted George Eliot and Charles Bray in their revolt against the nineteenth century doctrine that 'it all depends on yourself'.

THE EFFECT OF THE GROWTH OF THE WATCH TRADE UPON THE RIBBON TRADE

It is impossible to trace the many and minute steps by which these changes came about. The masters did not make their deliberations public even when they were acting in concert: the

PLATE 3.

34 Craven Street, Chapelfields: a journeyman watchmaker's house: front and back.

PLATE 4.

61 Allesley Old Road, Chapelfields: a master watch-manufacturer's house.

newspapers say nothing about workmen until they are on strike, and public opinion is a nebulous thing at the best of times. Nevertheless, foremost among the causes of change one may fairly place the introduction and growth of the watch trade. It may seem strange to treat of the watch trade as a cause of change in the ribbon manufacture, rather than to treat of it in its own right, but it is no outrage. It was an innovation, and from the moment of its introduction the watch trade pointed the moral of many of the arguments against the list of prices, for the skilled watchmaker earned high wages unfettered by any list.

Unfortunately nothing seems to be known about the early history of the trade in Coventry, except that it had been introduced by the beginning of the nineteenth century.[1] By 1830 the trade had taken root: it was characterized by the small number of master watchmakers, the variety of skilled journeymen, and the existence of a class of errand boys. Throughout the period from 1830 to 1860 the watch trade continued to expand, and by 1851 there were over 2,000 watchmakers. The demand for watches was less erratic than that for ribbons, and the watch trade never spread into the country districts round the city. Even with the most elaborate division of labour, the specialized tasks remained too exacting and too skilful to allow of the influx of cheap labour in prosperous times, and the consequent depression of wages in slack ones.

Weaving was not, whatever the weaver might say, a skilled trade. Of course there were skilled weavers, but it took skill to be a watchmaker at all. The natural result was that the ordinary watchmaker needed no list of prices to protect his standard of living, and it was generally considered that the husband alone in the watch trade, could earn as much as the husband and wife together in the weaving. Women were not employed in the watch trade, and the watchmaker's wife had time to attend to the cooking, to look after the house, and to play with the children. Most important of all, perhaps, in traditionally minded Coventry, the watch trade was organized

---

[1] See the *Coventry Herald*, 21 November and 30 November 1851. *The Resources, Products, and Industrial History of Birmingham and the Midland Hardware District*, ed. S. Timmins, 1866, article on the watch trade.

on a domestic and small workshop basis, and unlike the ribbon trade seemed likely to remain so.[1]

It is no wonder, then, that the working men of Coventry and particularly the freemen, regarded the watch trade as a superior trade. This superiority was not of a material kind. The watch-maker earned no more than a family of weavers: and the weaver and the watchmaker probably ate much the same food. The difference was that the watchmaker had his meals better cooked. It was the same with houses: the living accommodation in the watchmakers' houses being built in Chapelfields in the 1850's was almost identical with that in the weavers' houses being built in Hillfields in the same period.[2] Both the weaver and the watchmaker had in addition to the workshop, four rooms, two up and two down, but the rooms in the watch-maker's house would normally have been better scrubbed and dusted.

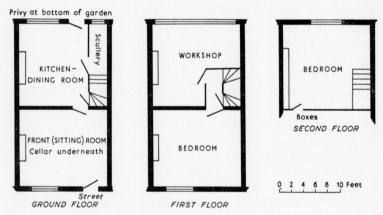

FIG. 6. 34 Craven Street, Chapelfields: a journeyman watchmaker's house.

There are, however, more subtle distinctions between classes and trades. Whereas, by the 1850's, the outdoor weaver needed a whole story for his looms, with windows on both sides of the

[1] Charles Bray, *The Industrial Employment of Women: being a comparison between the condition of the people in the watch trade in Coventry, in which women are not employed: and the people in the ribbon trade, in which they are employed.* A paper read to the British Association, October 1857.

[2] The details of the houses are from personal observation.

house to throw light to the centre of the room, the watchmaker on the other hand needed no more than a bench against a window. From this difference in the requirements of the men working at the two trades, there followed a difference in the construction of their houses. The three story weaver's house described in Chapter IV[1] can be compared with a typical watchmaker's house, 34 Craven Street (see figure 6). This house is an odd shape, being two stories high at the front and three at the back. There is a workshop with the characteristic long window of the homeworker on the first floor at the back.[2] The workshop is always at the back of the house. Evidently it did not matter which way the watchmaker's window faced— either north light or south light would do, provided one worked close to it. The watchmaker's workshop might face the sun, or it might not, but it never faced the street. The consequence was that the ordinary watchmaker's house presented to the street the appearance of a suburban villa, and that one had to examine the house from the back to discover that the occupier was in trade, and that he worked at home. It is difficult to believe there was no snobbery about this, and that this distinction did not in some way mark the superiority of the watch trade over the weaving.

But examination of the houses in the watchmakers' suburb of Chapelfields and in the weavers' suburb of Hillfields reveals an important difference between the two trades. Many people in the nineteenth century believed that the proximity of employer and employed was a mark of health in a trade. The larger ribbon manufacturers lived in or near Coventry, but not in Hillfields. One or two lived in Stoke, while others lived to the south of the city, like the brothers Cash of Sherbourne House.[3] Only a few of the smaller ribbon manufacturers lived in Hillfields. In the watch trade, however, things were different, and Chapelfields contains its full share of masters' houses. Along the old Birmingham road, on the northern edge of the watchmakers' suburb, are the masters' houses. Even today they

---

[1] See above, p. 75.

[2] One of the two bedrooms is on the first floor at the front of the house, while the other is on the second floor, at the back, in an attic. In some of the neighbouring houses the attic was used as the workshop.

[3] *Lascelles and Co.'s Directory and Gazeteer, City of Coventry and Neighbourhood,* Coventry, 1850.

give the area some of its atmosphere. In Chapelfields the houses are graded, roughly, from the masters' houses at the north end, to the smaller journeymen's houses with no front gardens, and the public houses at the south end. Chapelfields was an integrated and intimate community.[1]

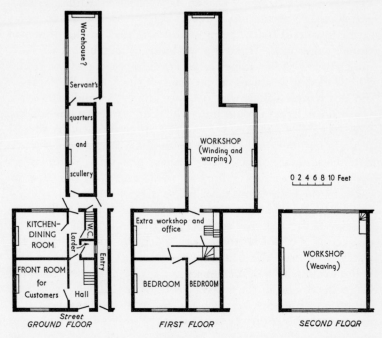

FIG. 7. 32 Queen Street, Hillfields: a small ribbon-manufacturer's house.

The way to become a master, architecturally, was to build a two story tail to the back of your house to accommodate your workshops. By the 1850's no substantial ribbon manufacturer would have built in this way, and only the small ribbon manufacturer, who had not the means to build a factory, or to employ

[1] Chapelfields also formed a remarkably isolated community. The area was completely built up in about thirty years after the land became available in 1845, and most of the surrounding land was not built up till many years afterwards. Although almost everyone living in Chapelfields was connected with the watch trade, not everyone connected with the watch trade could be accommodated in Chapelfields. There were watchmakers all over the old city, and there was even a small community of them in Hillfields, next door to the church.

large numbers of outdoor weavers, would have built such a tail to his house and gone into business in such small premises. In the watch trade, on the other hand, the equipment employed was so small that even an important manufacturer had no need to build a workshop larger than could be accommodated in his own garden. The length of the tail indicated the size of his business, while the number of sections of which it was composed indicated the number of times his business had expanded. Several of the large houses along the Birmingham road stretched their tails, after several attempts, right down to the bottom of the garden, two stories high all the way. In some of the other roads in Chapelfields several of the ordinary watchmakers' houses had little tails added to them, indicating that some specialist workmen, at least, were able to become small masters.

A comparison of one of the small ribbon master's houses in Hillfields, 32 Queen Street (see figure 7), with a master watch manufacturer's house, 61 Allesley Old Road (see figure 8), confirms the superiority of the watch trade. In each case the master lived on the 'servant level', and it would be possible to judge these houses entirely by the size and quality of the servants' accommodation. In 32 Queen Street it is makeshift, on the ground floor under the tail of the house, and separated from the back parlour where the family lived by an open passage. The servants probably lived and worked in the same room. In 61 Allesley Old Road, on the other hand, the servants not only had a proper kitchen and parlour, but bedrooms in the attic. Here there was clearly some division of labour among the servants, whereas in 32 Queen Street the servants were very likely maids of all work, who may even have helped with the weaving during the day, and eaten with the family at night.

In both houses the workmen coming in from the street made their way up to the workshop by a different staircase from that used by the head of the house. At the ribbon master's house, which is built right up to the street, the workmen came through an entry to a narrow staircase at the back of the house. On the first floor the master, having climbed his separate staircase, joined his workmen, some of whom went out into the tail of the house to do the winding and warping, while the rest went up another flight of stairs to the weaving loft at the top of the house. The watchmakers going to work at 61 Allesley Old Road, on the other hand, reached their workshops by the garden gate at the back of the house. The master himself could reach his workshops through his office in the tail of the house, without disturbing his servants in the kitchen parlour underneath. In the workshops themselves, the many parts of the watch, manufactured by the ordinary watchmakers behind their ordinary watchmakers' windows, met for the first time.

FIG. 8. 61 Allesley Old Road, Chapelfields: a master watch-manufacturer's house.

In each of these houses the front door led into a hall, but the watch-manufacturer's house had double doors. Visitors and prospective customers where shown into the front room. In each of the two houses one finds the same number of living rooms, but those in the watchmaker's house are larger. It would not have been unusual to have found in the watchmaker's house, in addition to the family Bible, a copy of Dugdale's *Antiquities of Warwickshire*, the current quarterly magazines, and technical literature on the trade.[1] The largest ribbon manufacturers no doubt enjoyed as high, or even a higher, standard of living. But the point, in this instance, is not to compare the standards of living of the masters in the two trades, but to compare the standards of living of the masters with whom the workmen came in contact. In the weaving it was generally a hand to mouth, and in the watch trade a comfortable life. This must have been a factor in the superiority of the watch trade over the ribbon trade.

In these circumstances it is not surprising that there should have been a drift of workmen from the ribbon trade to the watch trade. Nor is it surprising that this drift should have been most marked among the freemen. Apprenticeship was not obligatory, but it was certainly favoured in the watch trade, and while the ordinary freeman weaver was too old to change his trade, he could nevertheless apprentice his son to the superior trade, and so accomplish the change at one generation's remove.

The habit of apprenticeship did not fall off in Coventry during this period. While the population increased from 31,000 in 1841 to 41,000 in 1861, the average number of apprentices enrolled in each year increased from 216 in the 1830's to 331 in the 1850's. At this rate apprenticeship was more than keeping pace with the population. Furthermore the proportion of these apprentices going into the ribbon trade and the watch trade taken together remained almost constant, being 76 per cent in the 1830's, and 74 per cent in the 1850's. There were many fluctuations from year to year, but over the whole period the number of apprentices entering the ribbon trade declined, while the number going into the watch trade increased. In the 1830's 48 per cent of the apprentices went into the weaving, and 28 per cent into the watchmaking: by the 1850's 54 per cent became watchmakers, and only 20 per cent became weavers. Year by year through the fifties, more than fifty weavers, on the average, apprenticed their sons to the watchmaking, while one

[1] Verbal communication from Mr. S. Alexander.

watchmaker only, on the average, apprenticed his son to the weaving.[1]

These figures cannot be overstressed in telling the history of Coventry in the nineteenth century. The class of freemen by apprenticeship gave Coventry its character. Many of these respectable artisans were now forsaking ribbons for watches. Those who remained in the ribbon trade were trying to compete with the factories, and to go on working at home in the age of steam power. But the status of the weavers was being lowered in the estimation of the general public by the exodus from the one trade to the other, and in this way the watch trade was helping to bring the first-hand journeymen weavers to disaster. Subsequently, when the ribbon trade was dying, and the watch trade was declining in its turn, many of the descendants of these watchmakers found their way into the tool rooms of the engineering workshops.[2]

THE ATTEMPT TO MAINTAIN THE LIST OF PRICES

The struggle to maintain the list of prices in the period 1830 to 1860 gradually changed from an attempt by the honourable majority to make the unjust minority pay and accept fair wages, to an attempt on the part of the first-hand outdoor weavers to resist the factory system. The list of prices for plain ribbons was fairly well kept throughout the period, but serious trouble arose from time to time over revisions of the list, and over the prices paid for fancy ribbons. Important disputes occurred in 1835, 1840, 1842-43, 1848, 1854, 1856, and 1858.[3] In addition there were many minor differences involving small points of industrial discipline, like the strike in 1850 over the time of breakfast in one of the factories.[4]

When the list was being disregarded, the weavers' tactics followed closely the pattern described in Chapter III.[5] The offending master's hands struck work, while the hands employed by the other manufacturers contributed to a fund for their support. Meetings were held in the public houses if the weather

---

[1] The figures have been abstracted from the Register of Apprentices' Indentures in the City Record Office.

[2] Verbal communication from Mr. P. Avery.

[3] These are recorded in the *Coventry Standard* and the *Coventry Herald*.

[4] The *Coventry Herald*, 4 October 1850.   [5] See above, pp. 57-60.

was bad, or on Greyfriars Green if the season was dry and the number of men involved in the dispute ran into several hundreds. Handbills were circulated, and these, and accounts of the weavers' meetings generally appeared in the newspapers. From time to time one of the masters took the trouble to issue a notice, or to write a letter defending his conduct, or impugning that of the weavers. After a week or more out of work, the strikers appealed to the town in general, asking the Mayor to call a meeting and to promote a reconciliation. There is no need to recite the history of each of these struggles separately. Instead one can try to pick out the moments at which a change of attitude on the part of the masters, or of the men, or of public opinion, has taken place, and mark the steps by which the old industrial society was transformed into the new.

Many of the manufacturers, no longer believing in the list, ceased to come to the town meetings when the Mayor called them. As early as 1835 the Mayor had to adjourn a meeting because there were no manufacturers present. In the meantime he appealed to them to attend the adjourned meeting, which some of them did. Mr. Hennell then had the courage to state his arguments against the list. 'The lower our prices the more we shall sell', he said. It was not a new argument, but it was the last time that a manufacturer would take the trouble to explain himself to the town and to the weavers so clearly.[1] Time and again the weavers deplored the absence of the manufacturers from these meetings, and though they continued to rely on town meetings to test the sympathy of the public, from about 1840 the weavers' committee found it more profitable to wait upon each manufacturer in turn, asking why he objected to paying by the list. The answers they received followed a regular pattern. One manufacturer said he was paying by the list, the next said he would pay when the others did, while the third said he would never pay by any list. In 1843, for example the weavers' committee told the weavers on strike that they had called on the masters who were not paying list prices.

Mr. Merridew, who will not sign, but is paying above.
Mr. Cope, who will not sign, though he is paying by the list.
Mr. Caldicott, who will not sign, considering it an injury.

[1] The *Coventry Herald*, 6 February 1835.

Mr. Worcester, who will not sign, until a majority do.

Mr. Ratliff, who will not sign, and is opposed on principle.

Mr. Coleman, who wishes he could, but his profits are too low.

Mr. T. Brown, who will not sign, but will pay by it.

Mr. Dresser, who signed, but does not agree with all the prices.

Mr. Nathaniel Buckley, who will not pay by the list, but will sign if all the manufacturers do.

Mr. Jephcott, who will not sign.

and Mr. Ryley, who said he could not pay by the list in all respects.[1]

One after another the props of the old system gave way throughout the 1840's and 1850's. In 1840 Mr. E. Goode, an old weavers' leader, asked for his advice about tactics, said that he had never known a town meeting to fail, clearly indicating that this time he expected it to, and adding that he was no longer a weaver and glad not to be. His forecast was right, and for the first time, the resolution of a town meeting did nothing to bring the two sides nearer to a settlement of their dispute.[2] In 1848 another milestone was passed when the weavers were in dispute with Mr. Ratliff, and a fellow manufacturer, Mr. Caldicott, the Mayor, refused to call a town meeting when the weavers asked him to.[3] Yet another six years, and Messrs. Spencer & Horsfall felt strong enough to tell the weavers' committee outright that they did not care what the town, or what twenty towns, thought of them.[4]

Gradually, as the Magistrates and the respectable inhabitants of the town turned against them, the weavers were forced back upon their own resources. Their organization had been perfected during a couple of decades of strife: all that there was left to do was to make it permanent. In 1842, after they had induced the masters to sign a new list, or, as they themselves put it, 'put a right slap up top end on it', they resolved to form themselves into the Coventry Labour Protection Society, for the purpose of exposing any manufacturer or workman who departed from the list.[5] This organization seems to have applied to the plain branch of the trade only, and it was some months before the figured-ribbon weavers followed suit and resolved to form an association of their own.[6] These

---

[1] The *Coventry Standard*, 31 March 1843.   [2] ibid, 7 August 1840.

[3] ibid, 2 June 1848.   [4] ibid, 2 June 1854.   [5] ibid, 20 May 1842.

[6] ibid, 25 November 1842.

organizations seem to have been the first, apart from the benefit societies, to have had regular subscriptions and permanent funds. In the fifties these unions were supplemented rather than superseded by separate organizations representing the outdoor hands and the factory operatives. With organizations corresponding both to the types of ribbon woven, and to the conditions of employment, the weavers were always ready to call out the appropriate part of the trade, and to alter their tactics according to the circumstances, calling out as few men, or as many, as they chose. Finally, in 1856, as the division of society into capital and labour became more apparent, the different branches of the weavers' organizations were amalgamated into one union 'for mutual protection'.[1]

Throughout the 1840's and 1850's the weavers regularly employed a solicitor, W. Wilmot, to represent their members in court. Every so often when there was a strike, a union man would be sued for breach of contract, and Wilmot would be called upon to defend him. Every so often too, a weaver would sue his master for payment of wages. Whatever the case, Wilmot seems to have been there, and the probability is that he enjoyed the confidence of both the unions and the Magistrates. The latter, of course, could not recognize his services officially, but in 1851 the factory weavers met, 600 strong, for tea in St. Mary's Hall, to present him with a testimonial for his exertions in their cause.[2] Six months later the association of plain ribbon weavers, not to be outdone, met for a dinner at the Craven Arms, when they too thanked him for his services, and presented him with a piece of plate.[3]

As time went on and more and more manufacturers became Magistrates the weavers began to talk in terms of class legislation, and of political action. The terms of abuse used were still most commonly nationalistic—thus, for example, in 1854, at the beginning of the Crimean War, Mr. Hart was dubbed the Nicholas of Coventry.[4] But other terms kept creeping in: there were exhortations to unite the whole power of labour against 'them': the masters were 'base', and the weavers were 'noble', and so on.[5] These were something more than straws in

1 The *Coventry Herald*, 22 February 1856.
2 The *Coventry Standard*, 29 August 1851.   3 ibid, 21 November 1851.
4 ibid, 9 June 1854.   5 e.g. ibid, 3 September 1858.

the wind. Nevertheless, while some of the weavers were speaking in terms of class struggle, many continued to observe the decorous rules characteristic of industrial bargaining in Coventry in the 1820's. In 1842 the weavers deplored the action of some of their number who had paraded the streets with a donkey,[1] while in 1848 a deputation from Messrs. Robinson & Lynes's hands waited on their masters to acknowledge,

that they had adopted a wrong course in leaving their employ without the usual weekly notice, and wished to return [to work] for the purpose of giving a week's notice.[2]

This they did. In 1851, the operatives employed by Mr. Ratliff, who had been in dispute with their master often enough in the past, presented him with a cup,

in testimony of their approbation of his conduct in conceding to them additional time for the breakfast meal, the time stipulated for by the Act of Parliament being, in his opinion, too short.[3]

There were, however, less pleasant incidents to record. On the more lighthearted side, one may note that notwithstanding the vote of censure of the year before, the donkey was out again in 1843. Only this time, both 'Neddy' and one of the men who were leading him, were captured by the chief constable and six of the reformed police.[4] The power of the police, in fact, now made it impossible for the weavers to gain rough justice at the expense of their employers. Not even the new police, however, could prevent the weavers from intimidating their fellow workmen who preferred working to striking work, and it became increasingly common for the factories to be picketed, and for anyone who went to work when there was a dispute, to be 'followed' through the streets to his home. The more of these incidents there were, the more public opinion turned against the weavers' union and its committee. In the old days, when a majority of the masters had combined with the men and with public opinion to enforce the list, there had been no need to insist upon the solidarity of labour to the point of tyranny. Now that the weavers were being left to fight their battles alone,

[1] The *Coventry Standard*, 20 May 1842.   [2] ibid, 9 June 1848.

[3] ibid, 25 July 1851.   [4] ibid, 31 March 1843.

solidarity had become their only strength, and the weavers as a whole were becoming more conscious of the war between the two classes, masters and men, than the division of interest between the factory operatives and the outdoor hands.

THE GROWTH OF THE STEAM FACTORY SYSTEM

The rate at which the beliefs and attitudes of the people of Coventry were changing was increasing in the 1840's and 1850's as a result of the spread of the steam factory system, and of the nature of the outdoor weavers' opposition to it. Coventry had been in no hurry to adopt power working in the 1830's, and in 1838 two manufacturers, only, had employed steam power, with fifty-three looms in all.[1] It was only when the factories at Derby threatened to steal all the Coventry trade in plain ribbons that more steam factories were built in the 1840's.[2] The Ordnance Survey of 1851 marks six large factories, and another six smaller ones with engine houses.

From the moment the City Council adopted the Health of Towns Act in 1849, the plans for new buildings had to be submitted to the Local Board of Health, whose records make it possible to follow the fortunes of the factory system fairly closely.[3] Any factory constructed after 1850 would have been a steam factory, and nobody could have built a steam factory in Coventry in the 1850's without consulting the Board and submitting a plan. The Board's Inspector, Mr. Greatorex, soon reported Mr. Stephen Barnwell in 1857 when he started building a factory in Gosford without a licence, and made him conform to the regulations.[4] The full list of ribbon factories passed by the Board from 1852 to 1860 is as follows.

---

[1] See above pp. 48-49.

[2] George Hall, *Prize Essay*, 1861, pp. 15-16.

[3] The books of the Local Board of Health are in the City Record Office.

[4] There are, however, several difficulties about using the evidence from the books of the Local Board of Health. In the first place the Board kept no systematic record whether the plans which it had passed had, in fact, been carried out. Secondly, there is no way of knowing how many of the six factories licensed in 1850 and the one factory licensed in 1851 had been built by the time the Ordnance Survey was made in 1851. Thirdly, the entries in the books of the Local Board give no idea of the size of the buildings concerned.

Plan No.	Year	Description
284	1852	Factory in Earl Street for Mr. William Spencer.
315	1852	Factory in West Orchard for Mr. Townsend.
468	1853	Shops and Manufactory in Earl Street for Mr. Odell.[1]
—	1854	—
705	1855	Factory in West Orchard for Mr. T. Townsend.
787	1856	Manufactory in Much Park Street for Mr. Henry Dewes.
804	1856	Factory in Lancasterian Yard for Mr. James Hart.
811	1856	Addition to factory in King Street for Mr. S. Hammerton.
872	1857	Factory in Hill Street for Mr. William Eaves.
875	1857	Factory in White Friars Lane for Mr. S. I. Gilbert.
896	1857	Factory and dwelling house in Cox Street for Mr. James Day.
900	1857	Factory in Gosford for Mr. Stephen Barnwell.
960	1857	Factory in Much Park Street for Mr. Henry Brown.
—	1858	—
—	1859	—
—	1860	—

The most important point about this list is the large number of factories being built in 1856 and 1857, and the cessation of factory building in 1858, 1859, and 1860. The financial crisis of 1857 might account for the fact that no factories were being built in 1858: something more is needed to explain why no factories were being built thereafter. Throughout the fifties, the first-hand journeymen, the outdoor weavers, were trying to compete with the factories by building cottage factories. Psychologically, the origin of the cottage factory is to be found in the determination of these first-hand journeymen to go on working at home even in the age of steam power. Detesting the

[1] A doubtful entry which might belong to the list of cottage factories, see below pp. 97-98.

factory system as an infringement of their time honoured liberty to work when they chose, and despising the lower class of improvident weavers with no looms of their own, who had already taken work in the factories, they were determined to preserve their way of life, and their respectable, propertied virtues.[1] If steam was inevitable—and competition made it that—then they would not be driven out of their homes to work in factories. Why should they journey to the steam-engine when the steam-engine could be brought to them?

The details of the way in which they placed steam-engines at the ends of their rows of weavers' houses, and conducted the power with shafting down the row from one workshop to another, are given in the next chapter. Starting, probably, in 1847, the system caught on, until by the late 1850's the cottage factory was a serious alternative to the factory. Since these outdoor weavers used power, their houses became, for the purposes of the Factory Acts, factories, and the factory inspector was thus drawn into the homes of the first-hand journeymen— where the Acts had certainly never intended him to intrude. But this unexpected result was fortunate for the historian because the factory inspector, Robert Baker, while complaining about the burden of entering so many little factories in his books, commented on the cottage factory system with interest. In 1859 he reported that there were in Coventry fifteen large factories with 1,250 power looms, and that in addition there were 300 of these cottage factories, with anything from two to six looms each.[2] In terms of the number of looms worked the two systems were running neck and neck. But no more factories were being built in 1858, 1859, and 1860, and the cottage factory system was, for the moment, triumphant. The cottage factories were less efficient than the factories, and the reasons for their triumph were social, not economic. Before trying to explain the way in which the struggle between the factories and the cottage factories became identified with the struggle to maintain the list of prices, and how both struggles ended in the disaster of 1860, one must consider the origins and development of the cottage factory system more closely.

[1] e.g. Joseph Gutteridge, *Lights and Shadows*, &c., pp. 64, 149. The *Coventry Herald*, 11 July 1850.

[2] *Reports Commissioners, 1860*, XXXIV, p. 452.

VI

THE COTTAGE FACTORY

THE NUMBER, LOCATION AND ARRANGEMENT OF THE COTTAGE FACTORIES

ARCHITECTURALLY the derivation of the cottage factory presents few difficulties. Already, by the 1830's, some of the better class of home weavers were living and working in three story houses. Already, these houses were being built in rows. The adoption of steam power in the factories having to be matched by the adoption of steam power among the outdoor hands, all that was necessary was to place a steam-engine at the end of a row of weavers' houses, to conduct the power up to the topshop at the end of the row, and to transmit the power by shafting down the row from one topshop to another through the partition walls separating the houses.

From the moment that this was first done, a dual process must have followed: the conversion of existing weavers' houses to working by power, and the construction of new ones expressly designed for power. Robert Baker, H.M. Inspector of Factories, writing in 1859, said that the cottage factories had sprung up during the last twelve years, which would make 1847 the starting point.[1] But no more than a handful of cottage factories can have been built before the Local Board of Health in 1849 began to supervise the plans for new buildings. Since engine-houses added to rows of old weavers' houses counted as new buildings, it would be reasonable to hope to find in the books of the Board complete accounts of both the conversion of old houses and the construction of new ones.

Instead there is neither. The entries specifically relating to cottage factories are meagre, and a large number of cottage factories cannot be identified in the books of the Board. One might imagine that houses were sometimes built without the Board's permission, but this source of error can be dismissed at

---

[1] *Reports Commissioners, 1860*, XXXIV, p. 452.

once. Every so often Mr. Greatorex, the Board's inspector, reported that a building had been started without leave, and the Board soon brought the offender to heel. The inspector was doing his job, the Board was not going to have its authority flouted, and one must try to solve the problem in another way.

In the first place one has to reckon with the Coventry habit of adaptation. Where steam was to be taken to an existing group of weavers' houses, there was often no need to build a new engine-shed at all, for many houses already had sheds which could be converted. In this case one need never go before the Board with a plan. In the second place, the Clerk to the Board might note that a plan for houses, or a plan for houses with topshops had been passed, and forget to add that an engine-house had been approved at the same time. This seems to have happened in the case of the sixty-seven houses forming the great Vernon Street, Brook Street, Berry Street triangle.[1] In the third place a considerable number of cottage factories were erected in Foleshill, which was outside the area controlled by the Board, but included with the city by H.M. Inspector of Factories when making his returns. Finally, when one does hear of a steam-engine being erected, one does not know how many houses it was intended to serve. One engine might serve half a dozen houses, as in Edgewick Road, Foleshill, or sixty-seven in Vernon Street, Brook Street, and Berry Street, Hillfields. An entry referring to two houses and one engine does not necessarily mean that the engine was intended to serve only two houses. It might well have been meant for two new houses and a dozen old ones.

For one reason and another, then, it is not possible to build up a complete picture from the records of the Local Board of Health. The list of entries which can be identified at once as being likely to refer to cottage factories is as follows:

Plan No.	Date	Description
75	1850	For building houses with an engine in Earl Street. (This is the only certain entry referring to cottage factories in the old city).
—	1851	—
—	1852	—

[1] See below p. 102

Plan No.	Date	Description
—	1853	—
610	1854	For the alteration of houses and engine in Gilbert Street for Mr. James Lee.
—	1855	—
—	1856	—
892	1857	For three houses with weavers shops, engine house and chimney in Weston Street for Mr. Samuel Smith. (Plan rejected).
904	1857	For an addition to an engine house in Queen Street for Mr. Greenway. (Passed after modification.)
937	1857	For eighteen houses and an engine chimney on the Stoney Stanton Road for Mr. George Hemming. (Plan rejected.)
941	1857	For seventeen houses and an engine chimney on the Stoney Stanton Road for Mr. George Hemming. (Plan rejected.)
—	1858	—
1126	1859	For a boiler and engine house in Gilbert Street for William Ryley Greenway.
1140	1859	For five houses and an engine house in Paynes Lane for Mr. James Moore. (Plan rejected.)
1158	1859	For two houses and an engine house in Paynes Lane for Mr. James Moore.
1162	1859	For an engine chimney in Albert Street for William Inchley.
1184	1859	For an engine chimney stack in King Street for William Smith.

Several of these entries can only be shown to belong to cottage factories—and not to factories—after an examination of the neighbourhood concerned.

Clearly this list does not account for the 383 cottage factories which were on the books of H.M. Inspector of Factories by 1860.[1] No new cottage factories seem to have been started after 1859, though some that had been started before the trade collapsed early in 1860 were probably completed afterwards.

[1] *Reports Commissioners, 1861*, XXII, p. 446.

In order to find the 383 cottage factories one is forced to abandon the Board of Health's books, and go out into the city with one's eyes open. The houses built expressly to carry power look stronger than the earlier three story houses. They have taller topshops, and more prominent eaves. There seems to be no record of the older two story weavers' houses being used as cottage factories, and one can come close to the total of 383 without falling back on two story houses at all.

One naturally expects to find the cottage factories just beyond the limits of the Hillfields of the Ordnance Survey map of 1851 (see figure 9). Even if the first cottage factory was built, or adapted, as early as 1847, only a comparatively small number of cottage factories can have been built in the following four years. The entries in the books of the Board of Health at once direct one to Paynes Lane, Gilbert Street, and Queen Street. In the Paynes Lane area, there may have been from forty to fifty three story cottage factories. Bomb damage and redevelopment make it impossible to be certain. In the Gilbert Street and Berry Street area there may have been from 100 to 120: in the Queen Street area from twenty-five to thirty: and in the Albert Street area, to which both the books of the Board and the memoirs of Mr. E. J. Pollard refer,[1] from fifty to sixty. The Bradford Street area contained perhaps another fifty to sixty. The total for Hillfields, then, falls between 265 and 320. Foleshill, with eighty to ninety brings the total to between 345 and 410. Allowing for a few more, only, in the old city, there seems to be no great difficulty in meeting the Factory Inspector's total of 383 in 1860.

Tradition says that these cottage factories were built in squares, with houses on all four sides, and a steam-engine in the middle. This is how Charles Bray refers to them:[2] and this is how Mr. E. J. Pollard remembers them, adding that such squares were to be found in Albert Street, Berry Street, and Queen Street. The Ordnance Survey of 1851 shows how Hillfields had been laid out in the forties in squares, but these squares were being developed with two story houses before the cottage factory system began, and among the later buildings of the cottage factory period there is not one closed square corresponding to the tradition. There is an L shaped block, a

1 The memoirs of Mr. E. J. Pollard are in the City Record Office.
2 Charles Bray, *The Philosophy of Necessity*, 2nd edn., 1863, p. 410.

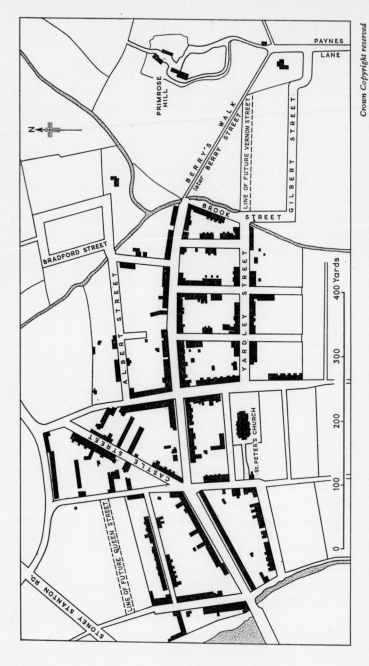

FIG. 9. Hillfields in 1851, showing streets and the extent of building, but not individual houses.

block forming three sides of a square, and a triangle. Furthermore, the triangle, the Vernon Street, Brook Street, Berry Street
group, must be the 'square' referred to by Mr. Pollard when he
says that there was a square in Berry Street.[1] The nearest one
can get to an enclosed square of three story houses seems to be
in Albert Street and Adelaide Street, and as Mr. Pollard was
living in Albert Street at the time of which he was speaking, he
may have taken his childhood memory of the square as typical.[2]
Both he and other people in Coventry have probably used the
word square loosely, to mean an enclosed space, in the same way
that Oxford colleges use the word quadrangle, and Cambridge
ones the word court.[3]

The cottage factories, then, were arranged to form an
enclosure. The shape of the enclosure was no doubt determined
by the land available, and by the length of shafting that could
be run off a steam-engine. It is easy to see how the existing
roads and paths, and the canal, determined the shape of the
Vernon Street, Brook Street, Berry Street triangle, and of Cash's
cottage factory at Kingfield. Each of these enclosures, whatever
its shape, formed a community of its own. From his window at
the top of his house the first-hand journeyman could see over
the little gardens of the community, and watch the other
weavers at work. Down in the middle the communal steam-
engine revolved—common not in the sense that the weavers had
clubbed together to buy it, but common in the sense that they
all paid rent to 'the proprietors of steam property' to hire it, at
a rate of two or three shillings per week per loom.[4] The noise of
the revolving shafting, and of the looms must have reverberated
all the way round the enclosure. In prosperous times it was a
sociable organization.

[1] Since there were no buildings on the other side of the street.

[2] The ribbon trade was on its last legs when Mr. Pollard was a boy, towards the
end of the nineteenth century, and he and the other boys at home used the topshop
as a bedroom. Nevertheless, there must have been work going on somewhere else
in the square, for he recalls that 'it was rather a curious sight lying in bed and seeing
the shaft twirling round above us.'

[3] There were several squares of older three story weavers' houses in the old city,
like Hertford Square, but these do not seem to have been used as cottage factories.

[4] The only references I have found to the ownership of the steam engines are in
the *Coventry Standard*, 29 June 1860, and in Robert Baker, the Factory Inspector's
report, *Reports Commissioners, 1860*, XXXIV, p. 452, and these are not very helpful.

THE LAST GREAT BLOCKS OF COTTAGE FACTORIES

From being built in rows, weavers' houses had come within a few years to being built in enclosures; and from weaving by hand, the outdoor weaver had come within a few years to weaving by power. Before the trade collapsed these enclosures were to be built on a very large scale, and it remains to describe the last two great blocks of cottage factories to be undertaken before the whole system fell into a forgotten backwater of the industrial revolution. These are the Vernon Street, Brook Street, Berry Street triangle, of sixty-seven houses, and Cash's at Kingfield, where one hundred houses were planned and forty-eight actually built. These two communities, one within and the other without the city, were the height and perfection of top-shops. Fortunately, each is well documented, the Vernon Street, Brook Street, Berry Street block from the books of the Board of Health, and Cash's from the diary of William Andrews.

The Vernon Street, Brook Street, Berry Street block was built in three stages, (see figure 10). The plans, which do not refer specifically to a cottage factory, can however be identified with certainty as Nos. 1040, 1119, and 1131, which were passed by the Local Board on 6 July 1858, for twenty-eight houses in Brook Street and Vernon Street; on 15 March 1859, for twenty-one houses in Vernon Street; and on 24 May 1859, for eighteen houses in Berry's Walk. All these houses were built by Eli Green, a ribbon manufacturer, who must have been a very wealthy man to have undertaken so much in so short a time. Eli Green was also, so tradition has it, a benevolent man, and when the windfalls lay on the grass in his orchard, he would pick them up, carry them to the front gate, and give them, one each, to the little children of the neighbourhood.[1] In addition, Eli Green was required by the Local Board of Health to make Berry's Walk into a standard forty foot road within five years and this he seems to have accomplished, despite the collapse of the trade. Berry Street is now an important inner thoroughfare of the city. On the south side of Eli Green's road stand Eli Green's sixty-seven houses, more than a century old, with the steam shafting still running across the corner from one block to another. The bricks and mortar are there: only the weavers have gone.

[1] Verbal communication from Mr. Walter Dunn.

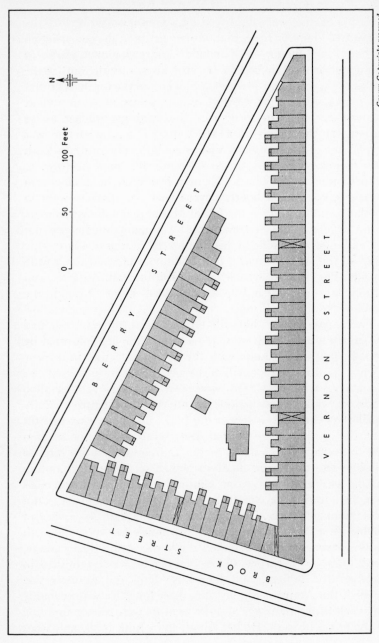

Fig. 10. Eli Green's sixty-seven cottage factories in Hillfields.

Cash's records were destroyed by a bomb, and it is from the diary of William Andrews that one learns about the construction of the cottage factory at Kingfield. Andrews joined Cash's as a designer as soon as he had finished his apprenticeship at the end of 1855. John and Joseph Cash, who ran the business at that time, engaged him for three years at a salary of £100 a year. He was sent to Paris to acquire the finishing touches to his training at the hands of a M. Vasselon, and while he was abroad one of the brothers came to see him. The brothers Cash were model employers; on one occasion they paid Andrews to go to London to see Charles Kean in *Richard II*, and they seem to have given him a holiday every year. In 1856 he went to Scotland, and in 1857 to the Isle of Man. Such holidays were no doubt exceptional—Andrews was a key man, but he was not the only one to benefit by his employers' kindness. On 6 May 1857 all the weavers had a half holiday, and went for a walk through Baginton to Stoneleigh and Bubbenhall. After tea and skittles at the Maltshovel, they walked home through the meadows by Ryton Bridge.

Two years earlier than Eli Green, the brothers Cash had chosen the site for their cottage factory in the angle formed by what is now Cash's Lane with the Coventry canal, in a piece of open country to the north of the city, beyond the revised city boundary,[1] where the rates were low. On 30 November 1856 Andrews walked out to look at the site (see figure 11). By April 1857 the houses were being built, and nearly six months later the brothers Cash invited Andrews to occupy one of them and to manage the business there. Andrews took a few days to consider this offer, and finally accepted on the understanding that he was to have £120 per annum, with house, gas, and coals free. In addition he was to be paid for any designing he did while manager there. The gas was laid on, Andrews arranged for his sister Anne to come and keep house for him, and with some extravagance he furnished the house with a dozen chairs, two tables and a carpet. On 8 October he was established in number 8 Kingfield, and four days later the business was opened. But Andrews did not stay there long. He was probably an overbearing manager, and the weavers were soon grumbling at the prices he paid. He left Kingfield in June 1858, and went

[1] In part of the former county of the city.

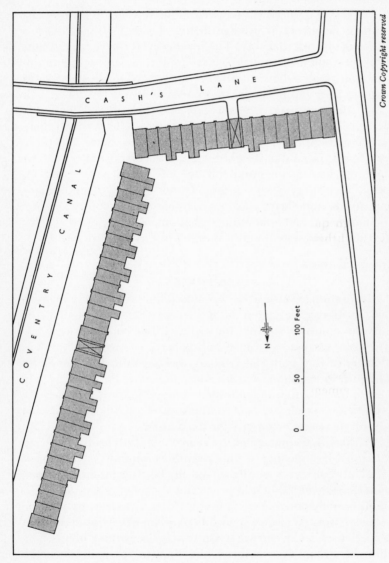

FIG. 11. John & Joseph Cash's 'hundred' houses in Kingfield.

to manage another part of the brothers Cash's business at Drapers Fields instead.

What had induced Eli Green and the brothers Cash to build cottage factories? It was probably the desire of the better weavers to work that way. The brothers Cash were benevolent, Quaker capitalists, and as good employers with a reputation for high quality figured ribbons, they were ready by 1856 to expand their business, and to do it in what was in Coventry in 1856 the ideal way. Go and look at the 'hundred' houses in Kingfield. The canal looks stagnant, and is idle. In 1960 there are houses opposite, where in 1857 there were fields: but there are flowers in most of the gardens, and the first two blocks of the hundred houses still stand (all but a few that were bombed), with their very early mock Tudor gables, their elegant buttresses, and their spacious, well-lighted topshops. They are a monument, and a monument that ought to be preserved, to a lost industrial system and a number of forgotten ideals.

THE THEORETICAL JUSTIFICATION OF THE COTTAGE FACTORIES

The brothers Cash were certainly influenced by the theoretical arguments in favour of the cottage factory system being advanced at this time by Charles Bray. Bray had been struck by the great extremes of riches and poverty in England, and had concluded that political economy was a cunning device, under the plea of paying a man his share in wages, for cheating him out of his birthright.[1] Unlimited competition had widened the gulf between rich and poor, and increased productivity had not meant increased prosperity for the masses.

At first Bray had sought a remedy in Owenism, and had attended the opening of the Owenite community at Harmony Hall in 1838.[2] Bray, who learnt too quickly from his mistakes, had entertained the highest hopes of this system of communism. Its failure taught him that communism awaited the development and education of a far more responsible generation than his own. Other experiences in Coventry in trying to help the working man to help himself ultimately convinced him that, in the mid-nineteenth century at least, the working man was incapable of conducting his own affairs, for the rather unkindly expressed reason that,

[1] Charles Bray, *Phases of Opinion*, &c., 1884, p. 58.   [2] ibid, p. 61.

PLATE 5.

b. Three of John and Joseph Cash's 'hundred' houses in Kingfield.

a. Part of Eli Green's sixty-seven cottage factories in Hillfields.

the people, like grubs, see little beyond the leaf on which they feed.[1]

If the people were unable to help themselves, what could be done to help them? To understand Bray's answer, one must appreciate the force with which he had been struck by the fact that, even when a man could produce more than enough on which to live, unless he could also exchange what he had produced, he must starve.[2] Men were not paid according to their labour but according to the demand for their product, and a brass button or a ribbon going out of fashion could reduce a whole town to destitution. Worse still, he foresaw that in a few years' time the whole of England would be dependent upon foreign markets, and that the nation's prosperity would depend not upon the volume of manufactured goods which she produced, but upon her ability to exchange manufactured products for food. The answer was to return to the past and to re-unite agriculture with industry:

Unite the operative again to the soil, and his own labour, applied to husbandry, will supply him with all the first necessaries of life, will protect him from undue competition, and make him independent of foreigners; whilst the surplus labour of himself and his family, employed in manufactures, will yield him every advantage which he can possibly enjoy from foreign trade. Trade—the only system that can be healthy and safe—is the mutual relief of wants by the exchange of superfluities.[3]

Owen had said something similar in the *Report to the County of Lanark*, and he too, in those days, had wanted the capitalist to take the workman by the hand and lead him to Utopia.

Bray had come to these conclusions about 1840, and by 1843 one finds him trying to put them into practice by joining in the great allotment movement of the time. To this end he and Joseph Cash founded the Coventry Labourers' and Artisans' Friendly Society, whose first object was to furnish working men with gardens. The Lammas lands not being available, the first difficulty was to obtain land. Landowners would not let their property to working men or to a working man's society, but

[1] Charles Bray, *The Philosophy of Necessity*, 2nd edn., 1863, p. 316.

[2] Charles Bray, *Phases of Opinion*, &c., 1884, p. 58.

[3] Charles Bray, 'An Essay upon the union of Agriculture and Manufactures', in introduction to Mary Hennell, *An Outline of the various social systems and communities founded upon the principle of co-operation*, 1844, pp. 55-56.

they agreed to let it to Bray himself, or to his associate, Joseph Cash.[1] The society had 400 gardens in the end, in Coundon, Brick Kiln Lane, Hill Street, and at one side of the London Road.[2] It was a fair number in a town the size of Coventry, particularly when one considers that the new houses being built in Hillfields had gardens of their own.

Bray's allotments prospered at first. Rent was paid in advance, and with each member paying a penny a week to the society, Bray was soon able to enlarge its activities. Boat loads of coal were bought direct from the pits, and the coal distributed among the members at cost price. Flour mills were taken, and a store was opened for the sale of flour and groceries. This was Coventry's first co-operative society, and a thousand of 'the most respectable working men' of the city belonged to it before the ribbon trade collapsed in 1860. When the ribbon trade collapsed, the society collapsed too.[3]

The object of giving every man a garden had not been solely to enable him to support himself and his family irrespective of the state of trade. There had been a second objective, which was to improve his health. As Mrs. Bray put it, in a book she wrote for schools about the British Empire, manufactures had created a large population in towns, divorced from the land, whose occupation

induced a large predominance of the nervous at the expense of the muscular system.[4]

Balanced labour, on the land and at the loom, would produce a healthier population. Mere agricultural work, so the argument went on, was very good for the physique, but it stunted the brain, and agricultural labourers were notoriously stupid. Weavers and other artisans on the other hand were noticeably more intelligent, but weak physically. In order to develop fully, therefore, a man ought to combine healthy, body-building work out of doors, with active, indoor work that made some demands upon his intelligence. The fact that in such a trade as Coventry's silk ribbon weaving, a man who went out

[1] Charles Bray, *Phases of Opinion*, &c., 1884, p. 64.
[2] From the annual report of the Society in the *Coventry Herald*, 1 November 1844.
[3] Charles Bray, *Phases of Opinion*, &c., 1884, pp. 64-67.
[4] Caroline Bray, *The British Empire*, 1863, pp. 34-35.

to work on the land would soon have hands too rough to handle the silk, did not worry the Brays.

Such was Bray's grand remedy. He dismissed the fears of Malthus, which, even if they were important, were not pressing. The world was large enough to feed everyone for a long time to come:

even with the present imperfect methods of cultivation, the labour of one agriculturist can support fifteen manufacturers, and, aided by machinery, fifteen manufacturers can produce as much as four thousand five hundred could in 1760, when each man's labour was sufficient for his own support.[1]

With land and capital, said James Silk Buckingham, who was for a time Bray's disciple, and with liberty to exchange with each other the fruits of their labour, what could possibly prevent the one agriculturist and the fifteen manufacturers having all they wanted? But Buckingham did not go on to suggest a visionary society made up of units of sixteen people.

Charles Bray, however, did see in the cottage factory a new vision of society. In July 1850, in a leading article in the *Herald*, he called attention to the experiments which had recently been made in Coventry in the application of steam power to private dwellings.[2] These experiments were bringing nearer his grand remedy of uniting the domestic with the factory system, and promised to realize

from their combination all the advantages of both. A range of dwellings, with lofty workshops in the top may be supplied with steam power at a moderate cost, and thus, while the husband and wife, or elder children, are employed together in a separate, well ventilated workshop, they are not subjected to the coarse jests, or low moral atmosphere of the factory.

One week later the *Herald* sensibly suggested that the workshops would be more conveniently situated at ground level, in a row at the back of the houses, but without mentioning that this was actually being done at Leicester on an extensive scale.

From this point it was but a step to advocating squares of cottage factories with steam-engines in the middle, and

---

[1] James Silk Buckingham, *National Evils and Practical Remedies*, 1849, p. 50, avowedly quoting Bray's sentiments.

[2] The *Coventry Herald*, 11 July 1850.

extensive gardens all round. In 1857, in his address to the British
Association at Birmingham, Charles Bray referred to the way in
which the cottage factories at Coventry were developing towards
this ideal. He expressed himself more clearly a few years later,
in the second edition of his *Philosophy of Necessity*:

making the best of the present system of individual interests, we may
see in healthy country districts squares of three hundred or four
hundred houses, with as much land attached to each house as each
man can cultivate, with a steam-engine in the centre of each square,
with power conveyed to each house to do all the hard and dirty work,
or to work the loom or other machinery. . . .[1]

Coventry never possessed a square of three hundred houses,
though it is said that the brothers Cash intended to build
three hundred houses in all, had the 'hundred' houses been a
success. Except for the visionary scale Bray's description is
applicable to what had occurred in Coventry. Kingfield and
Hillfields were both healthy country districts. The weavers did
not have as much land as a man could cultivate, but they did at
least have some land, where fifty years earlier they would
probably not have had any. Most important of all, the weavers
had power to work by, though their wives would have hastened
to add that the steam-engine did not yet help with housework.
   In these squares individual interests still triumphed over the
interests of the community. Charles Bray did not believe that in
the present imperfect state of society, individual interests could
be done away with, but he did hope that they would gradually
disappear, and that in time the squares would contain both
common and individual rooms for dining and working.[2]
H.M. Inspector of Factories, Robert Baker, who watched the
struggle between these cottage factories and the factories,
declared afterwards that, had the outdoor weavers approached
more closely to Bray's ideal, they might have been victorious.
Had they been able to subordinate their individual interests to
those of their square, they could have run their affairs co-
operatively, and become the masters of their own trade.[3] But
Bray had been right when he said that the weavers were not yet
ready to conduct their own affairs, and there were too few

---

[1] Charles Bray, *The Philosophy of Necessity*, 2nd edn., 1863, p. 410.
[2] ibid, pp. 410-11.   [3] *Reports Commissioners, 1861*, XXII, p. 444.

masters ready, like Eli Green and the brothers Cash to respond
to Bray's appeal to the capitalists to conduct the weavers' affairs
for them in their own working class interest.

Bray's theoretical basis for the developments in Coventry was
not original, except in so far as he re-arranged ideas common to
many thinkers. In industrial thought, as in philosophic argument, Bray was a great hand at combining other people's ideas,
and he was one of many who reacted against the industrial
revolution with plans for a return to the land. The smallholding
idea has reappeared with every economic crisis, only to
disappear, together with the smallholders, the moment prosperity returns. One need only cite the miners' settlements in the
1930's as an example. If one believes in the irresistible movements of history, then Bray's ideas were in opposition to one of
the most irresistible of all the movements of history. At a time
when the industrial revolution had enabled Great Britain to
rise head and shoulders above her rivals, Bray chose to hold up
as an example to progressive Britain, backward France and
Germany—the latter not even a nation. France, in her wisdom,
he said, encouraged rather than exterminated the class of
peasant proprietors. It was the same in Germany, where
twenty-six million people

consume less of each other's industry, employ less, buy less, sell less,
than four millions of our own population. In our social system every
man buys all he uses, and sells all he produces. . . . In Germany the
economy of society is directly the reverse . . . everything is made at
home.[1]

It was brave, but it was a voice crying in the wilderness. Great
Britain was not likely to reject her own unique achievement in
order to return to the position of France and Germany. On the
contrary, Germany and France were going to imitate Great
Britain.

At the best Bray's ideal society could only have lived a bovine
life. One may question, though, whether these little communities could ever have provided an answer to the trade cycle. What
would have happened to Bray's peasant proprietors if there had
been a bad harvest? Surely they would still have been at the
mercy of that unpredictable thing, the weather. There is no

[1] Charles Bray, 'An Essay upon the union of Agriculture and Manufactures,'
1844, p. 73.

way, in the English climate, of escaping the uncertainties of trade by throwing yourself on the ground and growing cabbages. It is only the industrial nation, where the division of labour is exploited to the full, that can build up the reserves needed to meet a bad harvest, by importing corn from another country which has had a good one. Bray's communities would have had no reserves. Salvation lay forward, not backward, and to say any more would be to argue where there is no more to be said.

VII

THE STRUGGLE BETWEEN THE COTTAGE FACTORY AND THE FACTORY, AND THE DISASTER OF 1860

THE OUTDOOR WEAVERS, THE FACTORY HANDS, AND THE MANUFACTURERS

THERE had been no opposition to the payment of weekly wages in the few large factories built in Coventry in the 1830's and 1840's. As one manufacturer after another built a factory in the 1850's, however, each one more efficient than the last, he was able to offer higher weekly wages, and to attempt to draw the experienced factory hands into his own factory. The operatives in the older works demanded an increase in wages, and if they were refused, struck work.[1] The trade being prosperous, these strikes were generally successful, and in 1858 the manufacturers stated that weekly wages in the factories had risen from 12s.-13s. to 17s.-19s. in five years.[2] At last, the manufacturers with the older factories and the older looms, unable to compete, proposed a return to payment by the piece, according to a list of prices. This was agreed, and for a while the two methods of payment existed side by side, piecework according to a list of prices in the older factories, and high weekly wages in the newer ones.[3]

Meantime the increased power of production of the factories had made it increasingly difficult to maintain the old outdoor weavers' list of 1835. Strive with steam shafting as he might, the first-hand outdoor weaver in his cottage factory was unable to keep up with the factories. Food cost more in the 1850's, and by 1858 things had reached the point at which the outdoor weaver must either accept a lower price per piece, and a lower standard of living, or else contrive that the prices paid by the factories were increased. Everywhere else, in every other trade in the

---

[1] George Hall, *Prize Essay*, 1861, p. 19.
[2] The *Coventry Standard*, 1 October 1858.
[3] George Hall, *Prize Essay*, 1861, p. 19.

country, the outdoor workers' wages had been, or were being reduced, by competition from the factories. The enormous scale on which this degradation had taken place in the textile industries in the 1820's and 1830's, had led to the appointment of the Unemployed Handloom Weavers Commission, and to the visit of Joseph Fletcher to Coventry in 1838. At that time the outdoor weavers of the city had still been prosperous. Were they now, in the 1850's, to be reduced to the miserable state of the country weavers in their own trade, and to the pitiful state of the cotton weavers in the Manchester cellars in the 1830's?

The outdoor weavers saw the issue quite clearly. In order to maintain their own wages, they must compel every manufacturer who installed new machinery to pay the same price per piece that they themselves received for the work done on their own, older looms. Throughout 1858, therefore, they struggled to impose piecework payment upon every manufacturer in the city, and to impose the list prices of 1835 by which they were themselves paid. Mr. Read,[1] a representative of the outdoor weavers, said bluntly that the establishment of a piecework system in the factories was essential to the interests of the outdoor weavers.[2] George Hall, who had once thought that weekly wages and piece rates could exist side by side, changed his mind, and became convinced

that the competition between weekly wages and a list, if persevered in, must either absorb all the best hands into the factories, or reduce them to the most miserable pittance of earnings.[3]

Finally Mr. Jephcott spoke for a whole class when he said that the factory system was one of absolute slavery, without finding it necessary to elaborate a point which he took to be self evident.[4]

It says much for the position still held in the city by these superior artisans, the first-hand journeymen, that despite the exodus to the watch trade, they were at first completely successful in their contest with the factories. Early in 1858, a dispute arising between the factory owners and their workers as to the difference between one master's price and another's, the outdoor weavers, interfering in a dispute that might have been

---

[1] Not to be confused with Mr. T. Read of the factory operatives; see pp. 126, and 133 below.

[2] The *Coventry Standard*, 22 October 1858.   [3] ibid.   [4] ibid.

thought to be none of their business, proposed a general return to the list prices of 1835 in all the factories throughout the city.[1] The factory weavers were apparently induced to agree to this proposal by the prospect of higher earnings, and by the false argument that all the advantages of increased productivity had so far found their way into the pockets of the manufacturers.

The masters paying by the piece at length agreed to pay by the list of 1835 provided that the masters paying by the week could be made to follow suit. By this condition the piece paying masters must have thought to gain either way. Either the other manufacturers would refuse to pay by the piece, in which case they would not be bound by the list themselves, or else, if they did agree, some of the disparity between the efficient and the inefficient factories would disappear. The weekly wage paying manufacturers would be forced in effect to pay more, and the efficient factories would be brought down to the level of the inefficient ones. With the piece paying manufacturers' promise in their pocket, the outdoor weavers now combined with the factory weavers, with the tacit encouragement of some of the piece paying manufacturers, to try and force the list upon the six important weekly wage paying manufacturers led by Mr. Hart, whose factory was the most up to date in Coventry.[2]

The operatives prepared to bring one factory out on strike at a time, and to support the strikers in the usual way with contributions from those who were still at work. The six manufacturers who were the target of these manœuvres showed unexpected unanimity, and replied with a handbill, addressed *To the Factory Hands and to the Public Generally*, saying that any attempt to bring the hands out on strike at one of their factories would be met by a lock-out at all of them. The weavers, undeterred, gave notice to strike at Messrs. Iliffe, Peters, and Hamer's factory: all six manufacturers kept their promise, and the struggle began on 4 September 1858.

Many of the weavers must have had grave doubts about declaring war. It was not in the interests of the men on weekly wages to strike, and from the beginning it seems to have been necessary to intimidate some of them into doing so. The *Herald*

[1] George Hall, *Prize Essay*, 1861, p. 20.

[2] The *Coventry Standard*, 3 September to 29 October 1858. George Hall, *Prize Essay*, 1861, pp. 21-22.

condemned the strike outright,[1] and the *Standard* was unable to
see why the two systems of payment could not exist side by side
as they had done since the factory system was first introduced
to Coventry twenty-five years earlier. Indeed, as the *Standard*
reminded its readers and the weavers, it was not many years
since Mr. Ratliff had wanted to pay by the piece in his factory,
and the workers there had gone on strike until they were paid
by the week.[2] Having blamed the weavers for their incon-
sistency, the *Standard* went on to remind them that many of the
outdoor weavers themselves, who were behind the move to make
the factories pay by the piece, were paying weekly wages to the
men and women employed in their own houses. The *Standard*
ended by touching a familiar note with the suggestion that, if
these labour troubles continued, the trade would leave the city
altogether.

The public opinion of the town, if not yet actively hostile to
the weavers, was at the very least perplexed. But perplexity was
bound to turn to hostility as soon as the weavers offered
violence to members of their own class. Violence to your
employer is natural: violence to your own class is not. Three
weeks after the strike had begun some of Mr. Day's hands who
had gone back to work were dragged out of their factory.[3]
Meantime many other weavers who wanted to work lacked the
courage to defy the union and its committee. The *Standard*
quoted the remarks of a factory hand's wife about her husband.

He got one and twenty shillings a week all last winter . . . while
hundreds of others had nothing to do, and he might be getting it
now, only he daren't go in. I declare it's like as if they hadn't got
common sense, not to let men go on with their work when they
might be doing as well as that. . . . I never seen the like to some
people—it's like as if they were fools to be throwing their time away
when they might be getting good wages and doing well. They seem
to be never satisfied without kicking up some bother.[4]

Intimidation touches society upon a very sore point. The
weavers' tragedy was that they could achieve nothing unless
they were united, and that the interests of the factory weavers

---

[1] The *Coventry Herald*, 10 September 1858.
[2] The *Coventry Standard*, 10 September 1858.   [3] ibid, 24 September 1858.
[4] ibid, 1 October 1858.

and of the outdoor weavers having ceased to be identical, unity could not be achieved without intimidation. But the Magistrates' reply to intimidation was bound to be prompt. On the next occasion when there was a dispute between the weavers and Mr. Hart, the Magistrates, three-quarters of whom at least were connected with the trade, warned the weavers against offering violence towards anyone who wanted to work, or towards those whom the weavers called

a skulking set of underlings, the muffs and duffers of the trade, who were making a harvest just now when it suited Mr. Hart's purpose to pay any sort of money to get . . . [them] to work.[1]

Things had now reached the point at which the outdoor weavers could not survive without these tactics, while the rest of the town could no longer tolerate them.

In 1858, as it turned out, the weavers remaining at work were numerous enough to support the strikers. In order to finance the strike the union rated the weavers who were at work at 1d. in the 1s. for factory weavers, and $\frac{1}{2}d$. in the 1s. for other factory operatives, and at 4d. for a hand loom and 1s. for a power loom in the outdoor trade. The strikers then received 7s. a week each,[2] and, after eight weeks five of the six manufacturers agreed to allow the Mayor to negotiate their capitulation to the weavers' committee, with which they refused to negotiate directly on account of what they called its indefinable constitution.[3] The sixth manufacturer, Mr. Pridmore, refused to give in, and prepared to brave the animosity of the union alone. Strange to say, he had apparently judged the situation well, for he continued to receive more applications for work at weekly rates than he could employ in his factory in Coventry. Accordingly, one day he hired a van to carry some of the surplus applicants over to his other factory at Foleshill. A few of the outdoor weavers, getting wind of this, attacked the van when it arrived. Mr. Pridmore's recruits brushed the opposition aside, entered the factory, and duly performed their first day's work. But when the time came for them to leave in the evening, the outdoor weavers were gathered round the factory in strength. The blacklegs were attacked, the constable was knocked unconscious,

[1] The *Coventry Standard*, 3 June 1859.
[2] ibid, 17 September 1858, and 12 November 1858.   [3] ibid, 15 October 1858.

and the windows of the factory were smashed.[1] Feelings continued to run high for some time after this riot, but neither side gave way. Mr. Pridmore never signed the list, and continued to pay weekly wages, while the weavers' committee, far from decrying the use of violence in this case, as it would have done in the old days, seems to have looked upon it with favour.

Although Mr. Pridmore continued to stand out, the other manufacturers had been forced to surrender. What had happened is, perhaps, without parallel in nineteenth century England. The outdoor weavers, terrified that they would be reduced to the level of the country weavers in the 1830's, had for the time being humbled the factory system itself. This is why there were no more factories being built in Coventry after 1857, and why some of the manufacturers who wanted to expand their businesses, were now ready to come to terms with the weavers' determination to work at home by building cottage factories instead. But the price of the weavers' success was that they had made many of the manufacturers as bellicose as themselves, and that they had gone far towards alienating the sympathy of the town. The masters' grievance was real enough too, for it was public spirited, surely, to raise the productivity of one's trade? Increased productivity, however, demanded lower prices and increased sales. If the masters who installed expensive machinery, and paid the highest weekly rates in the town, were to be forced to pay the weavers the same price per piece that they had paid before there was any machinery at all, then mechanization must stop, and Coventry give way to her competitors. The trade had reached a crisis in which both sides had reason to be bitter.

The outdoor weavers and the factory weavers had shown an astonishing unity. The piece paying manufacturers and the weekly wage paying manufacturers had shown a fatal disunion. United, the weavers had beaten the divided masters. But their victory was to prove a hollow one, for, encouraged by their success, they were to imagine they could repeat it. Meantime the masters seemed to have learnt their lesson, for they now formed an association of their own covering all the branches of the trade. As one manufacturer after another joined the association, the day of revenge drew nearer. One wonders how

[1] The *Coventry Standard*, 17 December 1858.

many of the manufacturers had signed the list with the same mixture of respect for one's pledged word, and agility in evading it, shown by William Andrews, the manager at Draper's Fields. Andrews had put his address after his signature, so that his signature would no longer be binding when he moved house. If this was the morality of the ordinary nineteenth century manager, one need look no further to see why the lists were never kept for long, and why the weavers could accuse their masters of bad faith.

THE GREAT STRIKE IN 1860, AND THE DEPRESSION AFTERWARDS

There was a massive sense of wrong on both sides of the ribbon trade by 1859, and both the masters and the workmen were ready to rush to arms. Next time, however, the circumstances were to be different, and the outcome not victory for the one side, or even really for the other, but ruin for everyone. On paper the victory would lie with the masters, but it was to be achieved at such a cost that the survivors would have little to be thankful for. Wars, however, have a habit of breaking out in unexpected places, and the shot that started this one was fired in Westminster.

Early in 1860 the rumour reached Coventry that the negotiations for a commercial treaty with France were going to lead to a reduction in the 15 per cent tariff on foreign ribbons. The Mayor asked Mr. Ellice, who had now represented the city for over thirty years in the House of Commons, whether this was true, and Mr. Ellice assured him that it was not. Nevertheless on 10 February the Chancellor of the Exchequer, Mr. Gladstone announcing the details of the Cobden Treaty, stated that the duty was to be taken off imported ribbons at once. The city had become the pawn of international politics, and her prosperity had been put in jeopardy for the friendship of the French emperor. The treaty, made in the name of free trade, was not even fair, as Coventry hastened to point out, for while French ribbons were to be allowed into England free of duty, the French were to be allowed to go on taxing English ribbons entering France.[1] This was a small point, perhaps, for few

[1] *The Speeches of Henry W. Eaton, Esq., M.P., and A. Staveley Hill*, 1869, pp. 9-10. The *Coventry Standard*, 10 February 1860. William Andrews, *Papers relating to the Ribbon Trade*, 1878.

Coventry ribbons would have gone to France, either taxed or untaxed, but small points sometimes rankle, and this injustice, and the way in which the treaty was made behind Coventry's back, go a long way to account for the city's continued distrust of central government.

It was ironical that the ordinary Coventry weaver, whose standard of living was threatened by this treaty, was, on the whole, with his radical opinions and Liberal vote, in favour of free trade—except, of course, free trade in labour. He would certainly, had he known about it, have supported the Chancellor of the Exchequer in his struggle with the Prime Minister in the Cabinet, for Palmerston wanted to arm against the French, while Gladstone wanted to reduce the army and navy, and to trade with the French, not fight them. This was one of the critical struggles within the Liberal party in the nineteenth century. Palmerston's fears were absurd, even if Gladstone's hopes were exaggerated. But Gladstone's confidence in the beneficial effects of free trade, does not excuse his failure to consult Coventry, whose support he took for granted even while he struck its chief industry a blow from which it never recovered.

In favour of the government it could be argued that the Cobden Treaty only completed a process long since begun. The prohibition on foreign ribbons had been removed in 1826, and after a slack period the Coventry trade had recovered. The protective duties had been reduced in 1846, and the masters and workmen of Coventry seemed to have taken the reduction in their stride. To meet the complaint that Coventry ribbons were of inferior design, the government had itself established a school of design in Coventry in 1843. After another seventeen years had passed there was surely no excuse for retaining protection. Either the Coventry trade was up to date, and protection was unnecessary, or else it was backward and needed a stimulus. The rest of England felt that the latter was true and that,

Coventry, as a town, is probably in a less satisfactory condition than any other manufacturing district in England. . . . Little enterprise is manifested by the master manufacturer, and still less by the operative weaver. . . . They seem to jog on in the old style in which their grandfathers pursued their trade, and to trust to foreign skill to provide them with new ideas, or to an indulgent government to continue . . . protection.[1]

On top of this there was the old argument that to go on protecting the Coventry weaver would be to go on taxing the English consumer. Finally, it was intolerable to think that any branch of the textile industries should need protection in the country which had started the industrial revolution in textiles.

The government ought to have known, but clearly did not take the trouble to find out, that the Coventry trade was too deeply committed to civil war in 1860 to be able to join in the crusade for free trade. The struggles between the factory and the cottage factory, and between the weavers who wanted to keep the list and the masters who wanted to destroy it, were now coming to a head. The two sides were not then, and never would be willing to combine to undercut the French. It was symbolic that the masters and their workmen now sent separate delegations to the continent to study the conditions under which their rivals worked.[2] Had the Chancellor of the Exchequer chosen to talk the matter over with the Coventry weavers, he would soon have found out the folly of his move. Was it contrition rather than admiration that made Gladstone send Gutteridge a gift of £100 more than thirty years later?[3] Gladstone was quite honest enough to have been able, after long reflection, to blame himself for his share in the disaster that overtook Coventry.

Although Gladstone certainly acted discourteously in not consulting Coventry, he cannot be blamed for all the blows which fell upon the ribbon trade at this time. He had no control over the Morrell tariff, which simultaneously destroyed the American market and intensified the battle for the markets which remained. He had no control, either, over fashion, which began to change from ribbons to feathers, or over the silkworm itself, which caught disease. Nor can Gladstone be blamed, when all these blows fell upon the Coventry trade, for refusing to repudiate the treaty he had just made. Despite the urgent pleadings of every Tory in the town in favour of a return to protection, there were such things as international good faith,

[1] The *Coventry Herald*, 11 March 1853, quoting from *Tallis' London Weekly Paper*.
[2] The *Coventry Standard*, 30 March 1860.   [3] See above, p. 14.

and the public law of Europe in the middle of the nineteenth century, and England had a moral obligation to honour her agreements, even if it was expensive to do so. The only question Gladstone might have asked himself was whether it was right for Coventry, rather than England, to pay the price.

The French took full advantage of the opportunity offered to them, first by the treaty, and then by the disruption of the Coventry trade throughout the summer of 1860, to capture a large part of the English ribbon market. The average annual value of French ribbons imported into the United Kingdom between 1854 and 1859 was approximately £1,000,000. Between 1860 and 1866 it was approximately £2,000,000, and before the war of 1870 caused a temporary setback, it had risen to over £3,000,000. In the same period the value of the ribbons made in Coventry had fallen from about £2,500,000 in the late fifties to less than £1,000,000 by 1870, by which time the Coventry trade was one-third of the value of the imports from France.[1] Throughout the 1860's, the people of Coventry, according to their politics, blamed either the Whig treaty, or the city itself with its labour troubles for the story that these figures tell. The trade declined steadily throughout the later years of the nineteenth century, and in 1960 only Cash's, and a handful of smaller firms remain.

The weaver, George Hall, says that the treaty only hastened a catastrophe that must soon have occurred in any case.[2] After Mr. Gladstone's announcement, the trade languished under the threat of French competition throughout the spring of 1860. Andrews's diary for this period is one long tale of looms idle, culminating in his own dismissal. Already, by April, there were said to be thousands of weavers unemployed. Trade being so bad the war about prices was bound to break out again. The *Standard* urged the masters to confer with each other and with the workmen about the future of the trade.[3] But the masters were only waiting to take their revenge. When the usual moves were taken to establish a distress fund, not one of the manufacturers signed the requisition to the Mayor to call a town meeting, and very few of the 'respectable' inhabitants attended

---

[1] William Andrews, *Papers relating to the Ribbon Trade*, 1878.

[2] George Hall, *Prize Essay*, 1861, p. 21.

[3] The *Coventry Standard*, 2 March 1860.

the meeting, or showed any sympathy with the distressed weavers.[1]

But it was another three months before the masters made up their minds to overthrow the list. It was characteristic of the time that they should have decided to do this, not by negotiation, but by force, and it is difficult to resist the conclusion that they wanted to humiliate the weavers and to teach them a lesson. Without any warning, the united manufacturers of Coventry, now forty-four strong, or as the weavers called them, 'the sympathizing bunch of forty-four', published their decision to abandon the list in a curt handbill, which was circulated on 6 July.

TO THE WEAVERS OF COVENTRY AND THE NEIGHBOURHOOD

In consequence of the recent remission of the duties on foreign ribbons, and the altered position of the trade from that and other causes, we find that it is no longer possible to maintain the list of prices to which our names are attached, and we hereby withdraw our names from those lists.[2]

That was all. The weavers at once replied with a request to the manufacturers to negotiate, with a view to maintaining the list, and lowering some of the prices if this could be proved to be necessary. When this request was rejected, the weavers felt that they had no alternative but to strike the trade, and a few days later every loom within fifteen miles of Coventry was silent.

The struggle upon which the two sides had now entered was fought with great bitterness. The small sum of money which had been collected for the distress fund was at once locked up in the bank by the trustees for the duration of the strike.[3] When *The Times* for 16 July gave a harrowing account of the sufferings of women and children in Coventry, many of whose husbands and fathers had been out of work before the strike began, the masters replied with a carefully worded letter, in which they explained that the trade could no longer support a list. It ought to be known, they went on,

that many hundreds of the people who are now walking the streets might be at work at wages varying—the men from 15s. to 21s. a week, and the women from 8s. to 14s., if the Weavers' Committee

[1] The *Coventry Standard*, 13 April 1860.   [2] ibid, 13 July 1860.
[3] ibid, 13 July 1860.

would let them. There are also many hundreds of looms with work in them, now standing still, because this same Committee, who are determined if possible to maintain old restrictions upon the manufacturers, have persuaded the weavers that it is in their interests to oppose projected improvements by a general strike, rather than to co-operate with their employers in adapting the trade to the new circumstances in which the commercial treaty has placed both masters and men.[1]

Any weaver who wanted to work, complained the masters, was immediately intimidated by a mob and by the fear of future consequences. Notwithstanding the protection of a large police force, the weavers were not yet willing to risk being branded as traitors to their class.

The men's views were as bitter as the masters'. They complained that the shopkeepers, their ancient allies, were refusing them credit. They complained that an official at the workhouse had insulted one weaver by telling him to go and join the army, and another by telling him to go and live off his fat. They complained, though with less surprise, about the tone of the warnings they received from the Magistrates against the use of violence. They complained that there was a policeman in every street.[2] As for the masters—they, of course, received the full force of the weavers' anger. J. L. of Foleshill compared the masters unfavourably with the silkworm herself. The worm consumed her own bowels to spin her cocoon, sacrificing herself for the good of the trade. The silkworms of Coventry (the masters), 'prey upon our vitals, and give us nothing in return'. He dismissed, though he did not answer, the masters' argument that the French could make ribbons more cheaply, and that Coventry could not compete with them while the list lasted. Were the French and the Swiss models for our imitation? Just because they squatted on the ground in hovels, and gulped their food while they worked, was the Coventry weaver to do the same? He protested against being continentalized. The list was a protection for the weaker weaver against his less scrupulous fellow. The master pleaded for free labour.

I repudiate the term. The weaver walks the street, his looms are standing, his expenses increasing; he learns that some incompetent, or some unprincipled, or some unfortunate workman, compelled by

[1] *The Times*, 18 July 1860.   [2] The *Coventry Standard*, 13 July 1860.

famishing circumstances, has yielded to the offer of the tempter, and taken the forbidden fruit, yet this is 'free labour'.

J. L. finished with a plea for the government to relieve the suffering by planting weavers' colonies on waste land, an idea reminiscent of Robert Owen and Charles Bray. He did not ask the government to restore protection.[1]

With feelings running as high as this the strike was bound to last some time. The vicar of St. Michael's, the Rev. S. H. Widdrington, the only parson in thirty years to enjoy some favour with the weavers, made an unsuccessful attempt to persuade them to return to work, on the basis of abandoning the list for one year, and reviewing the state of the trade at the end of that time. The weavers paid tribute to the good intentions of the vicar, but agreed unanimously that free trade in labour for twelve months would be free trade for ever. Only a few people supported the vicar when he put forward his plan at a public meeting in the Corn Exchange, and when a vote was called for the contrary, a forest of hands was immediately held up amidst applause.[2]

The strike was not to be ended so easily. Meantime the weavers, who had been accustomed to support the men on strike by contributions levied from the remainder, were beginning to feel the effects of having called the whole trade out at one time. Their own resources were slender, and the union committee now appealed for help to other trades and other towns, and especially to the cutlers of Sheffield.[3] But they only received £990 in contributions to their strike fund, and after the expenses of making their case known and appealing for help had been met, there was only £550 left with which to buy bread.[4] 18,000 loaves did not go far among as many people.[5]

In an attempt to get some of the weavers back to work, the committee went the round of the manufacturers, asking them

[1] J. L. of Foleshill, *Thoughts upon the Strike*, 1860.

[2] The *Coventry Standard*, 27 July 1860.

[3] Strike Committee Minutes, City Record Office.

[4] The *Coventry Standard*, 24 August 1860. There was a good deal of criticism of the committee's handling of the fund, and of their reluctance to publish detailed accounts.

[5] ibid. The number of people out of work over the whole weaving area was probably 30,000. The strike committee was only concerned with distress in the city.

separately whether they were willing to pay by the list. The answers they received were communicated to a meeting of the strikers on Greyfriars Green.

Messrs. Brown and Thomas will not sign any lists. (Cries of 'darkey— he was a weaver himself') . . . Mr. James Hart will not sign any list. ('We didn't expect he would') . . . Messrs. Franklin will not sign any list. ('There's your honourable masters.') It seemed the opinion of the deputation was that they might have done better with the old gentleman than the young one—he seemed inclined not to sign but to pay the price. The young man seems to think a good deal about his capital. (A voice, 'he'd got no shoes nor stockings a few years ago'.) Mr. Caldicott will not sign any list. ('They've got him in it at last, have they?')[1]

In the end some of the manufacturers engaged in the outdoor trade agreed to pay by the list and the committee decided to allow their hands to go back to work, providing them with tickets to exhibit in the lower windows of their houses, stating that they had the 'permission of the trade' to resume work. These tickets were regarded by the rest of the town as further evidence of the wickedness of the weavers' committee. Even the *Standard*, which still held to its opinion that list prices and weekly wages could continue to exist side by side, published a facsimile of one of these tickets and the editor commented that if anyone could supply from the dominions of the Pope, or the King of Naples, a more decided illustration of tyranny, he would like to see it.[2]

There were too few looms at work to support the thousands of people now faced by starvation. Consequently the committee's critics began to come out into the open. Mr. T. Read, of the factory weavers,[3] declared that he could no longer advise the factory operatives to sacrifice themselves for the sake of the outdoor weavers. An old committee man wrote a letter to the *Standard*, blaming the present committee for having made themselves so obnoxious that no manufacturer would agree to meet them, and no shopkeeper support them.[4] The *Standard* itself, which had been the weavers' friend for thirty years, published a series of leading articles week by week, entitled *Nuts to be Cracked on the Green*, referring to the wild and illogical speeches

[1] The *Coventry Standard*, 3 August 1860.   [2] ibid, 10 August 1860.
[3] Not to be confused with Mr. Read, a representative of the outdoor weavers; see above p. 114.
[4] The *Coventry Standard*, 24 August 1860.

now being made by the strikers at their meetings on Greyfriars Green. After three weeks some of the weavers in the outlying districts braved the anger of the remainder, and went back to work on the best terms they could get.[1] Some of the city weavers followed suit, and after eight weeks the weavers were beaten, and it only remained to find a face-saving formula for their surrender.

The Rev. S. H. Widdrington now succeeded at the second attempt in bringing the strike to an end. The weavers' committee having lost the confidence of both the town and the trade, the Vicar called a meeting of the strikers at which it was determined to reorganize the weavers' union, and to form a new committee charged with the duty of maintaining the price of labour in Coventry.[2] These were just brave words to conceal the fact that the weavers had no funds, and no heart for another struggle. The list was abandoned without a word said, and the true position was made clear in January 1861, when the masters agreed to negotiate with the weavers provided that no mention was made of a return to list prices, and the weavers meekly accepted the condition. But by the time the strike was over and the weavers were prepared to accept work below list prices, there was no longer any work for them to do. The weavers realized too late, that without the tariff on foreign ribbons, they could not afford the luxury of a strike.

The contestants had ample time in which to look about them and survey the cost of folly. While the weavers had stopped every loom in the Coventry district, the weavers of St. Etienne and Basle had been working overtime to supply the English market.[3] The masters had sought to break the list, and to establish free trade in labour. The list had been abandoned and was never to be heard of again. But had the masters won? For months many of them hung on before tottering over the edge into bankruptcy. There had been upwards of eighty masters when the troubles began. By 1865, when the smoke had cleared, and the casualties could be counted, there were only twenty left, and no fewer than fifty had become bankrupt.[4]

Meantime, in 1860-61 many of the weavers were going out

[1] The *Coventry Standard*, 3 August 1860.   [2] ibid, 31 August 1860.

[3] The diary of William Andrews, City Record Office.

[4] *Reports Commissioners, 1865*, XX, p. 466.

to the commons each day to work for 6*d*. and a loaf of bread.[1]
The relief fund which had been locked up in the bank when the
strike began, was now released. But it was a long time before
fresh contributions came in. The rest of the city seems to have
been disinclined to support men who were generally considered
to be out of work as a result of their own folly. It was not until
the winter set in, and the distress became so great as to render
inhuman any further arguments about its origin, that the Lord-
Lieutenant of the county, Lord Leigh, launched a national fund.
The Queen subscribed £100, her children followed suit, and all
the county families round Coventry contributed something in
1860 or 1861. Within four months upwards of £40,000 flowed
in. It was a handsome sum compared with the £990 which the
weavers had been able to raise on their own account while they
were on strike.[2]

The contributors to the national fund were celebrated in
verse by James Chapman, a weaver of Lower Ford Street.
Thanking them for their gifts, he nevertheless contrived to point
out that he had far rather they order Coventry ribbon. The city
wanted work, not charity, and the best charity of all was
Mrs. Scott's, who ordered a dress made of Coventry ribbon. As
Chapman put it,

> It's chiefly for ladies that ribbons are made,
> On them and their maids we depend for our trade:
> I'd thank each to wear on dress, hat, and bonnet,
> Some of our Coventry ribbon upon it.[3]

Robert Baker, the factory inspector, gave Chapman's advice his
official blessing.[4] One doubts, though, whether the classes

---

[1] See the preface to *Bright Sunbeams in Dark Dwellings, a tale of the Coventry distress,
1861*.

[2] The amount subscribed was recorded each week throughout the winter in the
Coventry Herald and the *Coventry Standard*. This fund was made available to weavers
over the whole district.

[3] James Chapman, *A poem on the Sympathy of Thousands of Friends who have relieved
the Ribbon Weavers of Coventry and District in their deep distress*, 3rd edn., enlarged to
seventy verses, 1861.

[4] *Reports Commissioners, 1861*, XXII, p. 397.
Another poem expressing the same sentiment, and recalling the better known
history of Coventry, was published in the *Coventry Standard*, 18 January 1861.

> Once on a time, when Coventry
>   Was pinched by want and broken down,
>   A lady of her charity,
>   Her suffering people's help to be,

that gave charity read either Chapman's verses, or H.M. Factory Inspectors' reports. But charity can take many forms, and not the least charitable people in the city were landlords like Mr. T. Soden, who made no attempt to collect his rents or to turn his tenants out.[1] Gutteridge, who was living in a house belonging to Mr. Eli Green, one of the forty-four masters who signed the manifesto denouncing the list in July 1860, was not asked to pay rent for a whole year.[2] It is as well to remember, however, that the landlords would not have gained much at this time by distraining for rent, for the weavers had long since sold their furniture and pawned their Sunday clothes, and new tenants would have been hard to come by.

As time went on and the trade did not recover, the weavers began to leave Coventry. Movements of this kind are generally ill recorded. But some idea of the displacement involved can be gathered from the census reports for 1861 and 1871. In ten years the population of Coventry had decreased by 1,555 from 41,546 to 39,991. As the table shows the decline was general throughout the weaving area.

| | Population | | |
Place	1861	1871	Decrease
Foleshill	8,140	6,638	1,502
Stoke	1,555	1,241	314
Bedworth	5,656	5,158	498
Exhall	964	907	57
Sowe	1,667	1,400	267
Nuneaton, including Chilvers Coton & Bulkington	13,046	12,421	625

Rode naked through the town—
And while that town preserves its name,
'Tis linked with fair Godiva's fame.

And now poor Coventry must pray,
A second time, for woman's aid—
Ladies in whom our trust we lay,
We do not ask of you today
The sacrifice she made—
Not wearing less, but wearing *more*,
Will grant the favour we implore.

[1] James Chapman, *A poem on the Sympathy of Thousands of Friends*, &c., 1861.
[2] Joseph Gutteridge, *Lights and Shadows*, &c., 1893, pp. 151-2.

Over the whole area the population had decreased by 4,818. When one remembers how fast the population had been increasing throughout the century, these figures become truly remarkable. They can be seen in perspective, too, only when one considers them in conjunction with the statistics given in the table below for the growth of the population in other towns in the Midlands in the same period.

Place			Population 1861	1871	Increase
Rugby ..	..	..	7,818	8,385	567
Kenilworth	..	..	3,013	3,335	322
Warwick ..	..	..	10,570	10,986	416
Leamington	..	..	17,402	20,910	3,508
Stratford ..	..	..	3,672	3,863	191
Birmingham	..	..	296,076	343,787	47,711
Hinckley ..	..	..	6,344	6,902	558
Leicester	..	..	68,056	95,220	27,164

The contrast could hardly be more complete. Nor do these returns show the full extent of the decline in the weaving area, because the exodus had almost certainly begun before the census was taken in 1861, and the population may well have begun to rise again very slowly before the census of 1871.

There is a popular tradition in Coventry that many weavers emigrated to the United States and to the Dominions. The telegrams received in the city after the bombing in 1940 seemed to confirm this. The official emigration statistics, however, are not detailed enough for one to make any estimate of the number of people going overseas from a town the size of Coventry. Many of the weavers probably sought work in Lancashire, for as early as the summer of 1860 advertisements appeared in the Coventry papers calling attention to the vacancies for weavers in Blackburn and elsewhere.[1] The weavers who went to Lancashire may well have found themselves on the move again a year or two later when their new trade contracted as a result of the cotton

[1] The *Coventry Standard*, 6 July 1860.

famine during the American Civil War. One wonders how many of the weavers went to seek work in nearby Leicester, whose phenomenal expansion began at this time, and how many others went as casual labour to Birmingham, which had been expanding so rapidly and for so long.

THE EXPERIENCES OF WILLIAM ANDREWS

Few of the weavers can have had experiences similar to those of William Andrews. Andrews had been dismissed before the strike began. Foreseeing a long period of depression at Coventry, he had resolved, in his own words, to be like King Alfred, and to penetrate the enemy's camp to see what he could discover. He inserted an advertisement in a Basle newspaper, had no replies, and not one whit discouraged, set out to find work in Switzerland. He travelled via Brussels, Cologne, and Mainz, stopping to look at places of interest, including the battlefield of Waterloo, on the way. Having reached Basle, he spent several days canvassing the ribbon manufacturers there for work. Meeting with no success, he gave up, and went away for a few days to look at the Alps. When he returned, he ran into a delegation of weavers from Coventry in the streets, who told him about the strike, and announced that they too had come over to see whether there was anything to be learnt from the Swiss. Andrews found work at last, and it was while he was in his first job abroad that he heard how the great strike in Coventry had ended in the abandonment of the list of prices.

This news did not encourage him to hurry back, and he stayed away from Coventry for eighteen months in all, returning in time for Christmas 1861. He took several jobs in Switzerland and then moved on to France, where he again tried to find work in the silk trade, in Lyons and St. Etienne. In France, however, he had no success, and he only stayed there for a few weeks before coming home via Paris. The trip had done much to broaden his mind, and nothing to diminish his sense of his own ability. His comment on returning to Coventry was that everything looked much smaller than it used to do; only the churches were the same. Andrews went straight to his old employers, the Cash's, and asked for work. They were able, despite the state of the trade, to take him back as a designer, at a salary of £100 a year. This, as Andrews noted with disgust in his diary, was the same salary at which he had first started work there six years before.

Andrews had recorded in his diary, in 1856-57, the building of the cottage factory at Kingfield. Now, on his return, he was able to record its failure. He found that a way had been knocked through the partition walls from one shop to another, and that the top story of each of the two blocks was now run as a factory. The weavers might still be working above their own houses, but they were no longer working at home. They still made their way up to the factory through their own trap doors, but soon these were to be closed, and the weavers would have to proceed to the factory by leaving their own houses, and walking through the yard to the external iron staircase in the corner between the two blocks.[1]

Andrews found John and Joseph Cash much changed. He thought that the collapse of the trade had made them more exacting. It was no wonder. The brothers Cash had done nothing to bring about the crisis, but they had suffered with all the rest. Andrews had the honesty to record that he too had changed, and the straitened circumstances of the brothers Cash and Andrews' increased self-confidence account for the fact that it was not long before employers and employee fell out. Within a few weeks the brothers Cash asked Andrews to supervise the business at Kingfield, which he had already managed once before, when it was opened in 1857. After some hesitation Andrews agreed, but this time he refused to go and live there. This was perhaps a mistake, because he was living in his father's house in the city, and had to get up at five o'clock in the morning in order to walk over to Kingfield before work began at six. It was often seven o'clock before he got home in the evenings, and the long hours, and the difficulty of sleeping for fear of being late in the mornings began to affect his temper, if not his health. After an argument with Joseph Cash he was given a month's notice to leave. When the time came, Andrews meticulously paid the hands, balanced the accounts, put tickets on all the silk, closed the establishment at the proper time, and sent the key to Mr. John Cash in an envelope. They parted more polite than friendly. Andrews soon found work with Messrs. Dalton & Barton, and ultimately went into business on his own.

[1] Verbal communication from Mr. Walter Dunn.

THE END OF THE COTTAGE FACTORIES

The brothers Cash had had to abandon home working for the severer discipline and more effective supervision of the factory. With these changes they were still able to keep the weavers at Kingfield at work, at a time when many of the cottage factories were not working at all. Like many other people in Coventry, the brothers Cash had found that the cottage factory was not well fitted to survive a recession, for when some of the weavers had work, and the others had not, the engine had to be started, and the shafting revolved, just as though there were work for all of them. Many of the occupiers of the cottage factories in Coventry complained in 1860-61 that they had to pay for the steam when they had no work to do. Finally, 'the proprietors of steam property' agreed that a weaver who had no work for his looms should not be charged for steam, though they continued to charge the weaver with two looms, and work for only one of them, the rent of steam for two. The weavers did not agree that this was just, but they had no alternative but to pay.[1]

Making his annual report in March 1861, Robert Baker, the factory inspector, said that he had visited the 383 cottage factories on his list, and that only 198 remained tenanted as they had been one year earlier. Eighty-three were occupied by new tenants, twenty-five were vacant, sixty-eight had reverted to hand power, and nine were altogether idle.[2] It was a depressing picture, and quite the worst feature of it was the reversion to hand power.[3] The practice had originated in the 1850's, when the cottage factories were being constructed, and the weavers had sometimes employed boys to turn their looms for a few weeks before the steam shafting was finished. The system had been condemned then by Mr. T. Read, of the factory operatives, who had alleged that the boys were sometimes worked from five in the morning until eleven at night.[4] In the depressed state of the trade in the 1860's, when the power had been disconnected from some of the blocks of cottage factories altogether,

---

[1] The *Coventry Standard*, 6 July 1860.

[2] *Reports Commissioners, 1861*, XXII, p. 446.   [3] ibid, *1864*, XXII, p. 758.

[4] The *Coventry Standard*, 10 September 1858. Mr. T. Read, see above, p. 126, note 3.

the system threatened to become permanent. The boy's labour according to Karl Marx, was now worse than it had been before. Formerly the steam-engine had replaced the boy: now the boy was replacing the steam-engine.[1] This was a mere play with words. The boy received even lower wages than he had done before, but this was true of everyone in the trade, and there is no evidence that his work was any worse than it had ever been. This is not to condone the system, whose worst feature was that the boy was unprotected by law. The moment a cottage factory ceased to be worked by steam power it ceased for the purposes of the Act to be a factory, and the Factory Acts did not yet apply to hand labour of this kind.

The factory inspector who passed through the homes of the first-hand outdoor weavers to reach the cottage factories above, had ample opportunity to talk to the members of this self-reliant class and to their families, and to learn their aspirations and their weaknesses. Their tragedy was that they were just a little bit more willing to resent factory work than they were able to compete with the factories at home, and that they were just a little bit more willing to believe that their masters took more than their share of the joint product than they were able to supply the masters' places. These men of property had too little property for an age in which the significant unit of production had become the factory rather than the loom. In the old industrial system the owning of a loom raised the first-hands to the position of a superior class. In the new system their looms were a burden to them. If they were to have maintained their superior standard of living, they ought to have managed their cottage factories co-operatively, or gone into the factories gladly and made them their own.[2]

In 1859 Robert Baker had entertained great hopes of the cottage factory system, thinking that it would re-transfer labour from the factory to the home.[3] But six years later he was able to pronounce its death:

it has long been a struggle for the mastery, as it were, between the cottage factory and the factory *per se*: and it has been interesting to look on and see how it might end. . . . It is . . . now beginning to be tolerably obvious . . . that, though the cottage loom lingers on a

---

[1] Karl Marx, *Capital*, Everyman, 1930, Vol. 1, p. 522, note 2.

[2] *Reports Commissioners, 1861*, XXII, p. 443 seq.   [3] ibid, *1860*, XXXIV, p. 452.

little after the most disastrous experiences, it is more perhaps, on account of the capital which remains invested in it, and in the buildings which have been specially erected for it, than as to any doubt of its being eventually superseded.[1]

The cottage factory, like the trade, was lingering ere it died. The blow, as one commentator said, had fallen most heavily on those who had worked hard and been distinguished for their provident habits.[2] It was ironical that the class for whom the cottage factories had been built possessed all the qualities of sturdy independence, and respect for property that Victorian England would, in other circumstances, have valued most.

[1] *Reports Commissioners, 1866,* XXIV, p. 314.
[2] In the preface to *Bright Sunbeams in Dark Dwellings,* anon., 1861.

EPILOGUE

MANY more studies of single towns will have to be made before Coventry can find its place in a synthesis of English town life during the industrial revolution. Enough work has, however, already been done to make it possible to compare Coventry with Nottingham and Leicester, two other Midland, medieval and incorporated towns.[1] The inhabitants of the three towns worked at similar trades. Nottingham and Leicester (together with Derby) were centres of the hosiery, stocking knitting, or framework knitting trade, which was carried on in the garrets of the urban artisans and in the parlours of the country cottages of the surrounding areas. In the hosiery trade, as in the ribbon trade, there is clear evidence, from 1770 onwards, of the attempt to establish and maintain a list of prices. The hosiery trade, like the ribbon trade, gave rise to a class of undertakers, and was only converted to working by power about the middle of the nineteenth century. Neither trade enjoyed a clear superiority over its foreign rivals, and Nottingham and Leicester did little more than Coventry to support Manchester's crusade for free trade.

At the beginning of the nineteenth century, then, there was an apparent similarity between the ribbon trade in Coventry and the hosiery trade in Nottingham and Leicester. But there was this difference between them. In Coventry the old system, with its list of prices and its apprenticeships, was still working, and was to survive the assaults of the first half of the century, but in Nottingham and Leicester the old system never had worked well, and by 1820 it had broken down altogether. This may be attributed largely, but not entirely, to the differences in the organization of the two trades. The silk trade as a whole enjoyed monopoly conditions, and the various branches had become identified with different towns—Spitalfields, Macclesfield, Leek, and Derby as well as Coventry, while the masters in the various branches of the trade and in the different towns showed

[1] See A. Temple Patterson, *Radical Leicester*, 1954, Duncan Gray, *Nottingham —Settlement to City*, 1953, and F. A. Wells, *History of the Midland Hosiery Trade*, 1935.

little disposition to invade each other's provinces. Although the masters in Derby did at one time threaten to enter the Coventry trade in fancy ribbons, the general rule was a producers' paradise in which they let each other be. The ribbon trade being shared between Coventry and Derby, and the Coventry trade being confined to a definite area, it was comparatively easy for the ribbon weavers to rally the public opinion of the town which preferred good wages to high poor rates.

In the hosiery trade it was different. The very existence of Leicester made it difficult to impose agreed wages and conditions of work in Nottingham and vice versa. Not only was the stocking trade spread over a greater area than the ribbon weaving, with more than one main centre of production, but stockings were made of more than one raw material. Ribbons were made of silk, but stockings were made of cotton, worsted, and silk, and although these three branches of the trade were concentrated to some extent in Nottingham, Leicester, and Derby respectively, the possibilities for overlapping were endless. There was a great variety of ribbons, but there was already an almost infinite variety of stockings before Heathcoat in 1823 showed how the stocking frame could be adapted to knit lace, and joined two whole industries together overnight. In these circumstances it was difficult for the framework knitters to win the support of the general public, and when they themselves combined to strike work, this was a sign not of their strength, but of their desperation. To strike the whole trade, in Nottingham and Leicester in 1817 and 1819, as in Coventry in 1860, was a sign that the old system had broken down, and that society as a whole had failed.

But the differences between Coventry and Nottingham and Leicester cannot be ascribed wholly to the differences in the organization of the two trades—otherwise the list of prices would have survived in other silk-weaving towns like Spitalfields and Macclesfield. There was a political factor too: Coventry, Nottingham, and Leicester all returned Members of Parliament to the old House of Commons, but in Nottingham and Leicester the franchises were narrow, and the county families intervened successfully in the politics of the city. Coventry was a city apart: there was no Duke of Newcastle or Duke of Rutland to subordinate the city to the aristocracy, while the wide and working class franchise also disarmed both Chartism, which appealed strongly to hand-loom weavers and framework knitters elsewhere, and the political agitation born of Dissent, which became such a powerful factor in Manchester and Birmingham. The franchise saved the working classes of Coventry both from the division of energies evident in Leicester, where radical agitation turned from fair wages to the suffrage and back again, doing very little to achieve either, and from the Chartist delusion that full employment would somehow follow automatically upon universal suffrage. In Coventry it was the workmen who kept their masters out of politics: it was a salutary balance of power, which substituted an element of mutual respect for the mutual suspicion of Nottingham and Leicester, where, in the early nineteenth century, both politics and industrial disputes were more violently contested than in Coventry. Coventry, which had no Chartism, had no Luddism either, and Mr. Beck's factory was not burned down by a secret society of masked men terrorizing a whole countryside.[1] A wide franchise and a small town put the working class on a level with other classes, and created circumstances in which the whole community concerned itself with the conditions of employment.

In Coventry these circumstances changed, and the industrial revolution occurred, when the ribbon trade was opened to capitals of all sizes, the masters became Magistrates, and free trade in labour was substituted for the list of prices. The industrial revolution in Coventry did not occur either as a result of the invention of the steam-engine, or as a result of the subsequent revolution in transport. Technological innovation was only one of the factors involved in what was primarily a sociological change in the intricate relationships of town and trade. In Coventry at least Arnold Toynbee was right when he defined the industrial revolution as the substitution of competition for the medieval regulations which had previously controlled the production and distribution of wealth. When this happened the ground was prepared for class war and the substitution of a Labour for a Liberal party.

There are many aspects of Coventry society about which one would like to know more. Far too little is known about the landlords to the south and to the north of Coventry, and about

---

[1] See above, p. 48.

the attitudes of the masters towards both profits and religion. The names of the union leaders are recorded in the newspapers, but nothing is known about their lives. We do not even know the names of the 'proprietors of steam property'.[1] Some of the details, therefore, are far from clear, but one dominant, and personal impression remains. This is that the condition of the ribbon weavers and of their masters in the period 1820-60 is best described by an abstract concept used by political philosophers—the state of nature. This was the term used by both Locke and Hobbes in England in the seventeenth century to describe the predicament in which human beings are placed when they are without government.

Locke says that in a state of nature most men are good, and goes on to add that, notwithstanding their goodness, the state of nature has certain disadvantages. If all men were good, so the assumption runs, government would be unnecessary. Equally well, if all men were bad, government would be impossible. In fact, because a few men are bad, the idyllic state of nature, of peace and mutual confidence, which Locke regards as natural to man, tends always to deteriorate, until Locke's state of nature is no better than Hobbes's natural state of war. This is generally held to be a weakness in Locke's *Second Treatise on Civil Government*. Far from being its weakness, however, this is its strength. This alone provides the key to the nature of man's predicament, and to its solution, as Locke sees it, and as it existed in the ribbon trade in Coventry in the nineteenth century.

At the beginning of the nineteenth century the trade in Coventry had been regulated as effectively by the ten or twelve old masters, and by the public opinion of the town, as it could ever have been by a formally constituted parliament. Round about the end of the Napoleonic wars this system broke down, and the trade fell back into a state of nature during the 1820's and 1830's. When this happened, a large majority of the masters and of the men continued to behave well, neither offering to pay, nor accepting too low a wage. Unfortunately, the few bad masters and bad men, having passed beyond the effective control of the majority, were always tending, as the natural result of competition, to bring the good majority down to their own level.

[1] See above, pp. 101, 133.

By 1830 the masters and workmen of Coventry had returned to a Lockeian state of nature. Had they been encouraged by the government at Westminster, they would still have been capable of governing the trade themselves, because the good majority, being moved by right reason, were perfectly well able to agree on what constituted a just price. Unfortunately, the government at Westminster, better versed in the theories of Adam Smith than in those of John Locke, thought that any attempt to regulate a trade must end in a conspiracy against the public, and refused to co-operate with them to re-establish government in the ribbon trade. Consequently, the problem facing the masters and workmen lay, not in defining what was just, but in enforcing justice. The longer the few bad masters and the few bad workmen were allowed to drag the majority down towards their own level, the more closely the condition of the trade corresponded to Hobbes's natural state of war. By 1858 Hobbes's description of the state of nature fitted the Coventry ribbon trade more closely than Locke's, and a much greater effort of will, or of force, was necessary if government was to be re-established.

Industry always corresponds more or less closely to the states of nature envisaged by Locke and Hobbes, and nothing is more difficult than to substitute a state of government for a state of nature. Governments are not established overnight, as the analogies of the political theorists might lead us into thinking. God does not establish peace in industry by divine writ, and hundreds of years of human effort, offset by whole decades of backsliding have not been sufficient to complete the task. The state of nature continues to exist where it has always existed, within political societies. Men in industry are always striving to bring the state of nature to an end, but their attempts to do so must often be, and can always be represented to be, a brake on technical progress and a threat to the consumer. The difficulty in a democracy is to decide how high a price the community as a whole can afford to pay for the desirable object of letting the masters and men in different trades govern themselves.

APPENDIX

THE HISTORICAL VALUE OF *MIDDLEMARCH*

Persons and incidents in *Middlemarch* are not taken straight from life, nor, on the other hand, are they wholly fanciful. Charles Bray, a ribbon-manufacturer, yet recognized himself in Mr. Brooke, a landowner, but a 'leaky minded fool', and a man of 'miscellaneous opinions, acquiescent temper, and uncertain vote'. Lydgate has been identified by A. T. Kitchel, in *Quarry for Middlemarch*, as Dr. Albutt, a man of Leeds, not Coventry, but modified, perhaps, by Coventry's Dr. Bury, who looked after George Eliot's father in his last illness, or Edward Clarke, a surgeon at Meriden, who married her sister Christiana.

The struggle between the Middlemarch Infirmary and the New Fever Hospital is not an accurate history of the struggle in Coventry between the provident hospital and the charitable one, but at many points it would pass for one. There is an unmistakeable likeness too, between George Eliot's description of Ladislaw coming to edit the *Pioneer* for Mr. Brooke, and Charles Bray's description in his autobiography of the young, would-be editor of the *Herald*, who strutted up and down the lawn at Rosehill, reciting, to prove his fitness for the post.

Where one can identify the incidents which suggested those in *Middlemarch* one should not rely absolutely upon their having taken place in 1830-32. George Eliot has taken careful liberties with time—nowhere more carefully than with the three illnesses which play so important a part in the plot, Fred Vincy's typhoid fever, Casaubon's heart disease, and Raffles's delirium tremens. This is explained at some length by A. T. Kitchel.

Middlemarch itself is Coventry, an identification that is easy to assert, but which it is not quite so easy to prove. Coventry was, however, not only the only provincial silk ribbon making town where the surveyors were laying out a railway in the period 1830-32, but also the only town where, before the great Reform Bill, the elections were fought between light and dark blue factions and the results determined by the freemen. It was, furthermore, the only town, barring Nuneaton, that George Eliot knew intimately enough to write about at such length. Indeed, when one considers George Eliot's life, one can fairly argue that Middlemarch could not have been anywhere else. For a description of Nuneaton, one should turn to Treby Magna in *Felix Holt*.

The other places in the story are Lowick, an agricultural village, and Tipton and Freshitt, where there was weaving. In her notes for *Middlemarch* George Eliot drew a diagram to show Lowick two miles on one side of Middlemarch, and Tipton and Freshitt three miles on the other. In *Middlemarch*, Lowick is described not as two, but as less than three miles from Middlemarch. Weaving being confined to the north of the city, Lowick, with no weaving must have been to the south. Two miles away from Coventry is Stivichall: just under three miles as the crow flies is Baginton. Mr. Brooke calls on Dorothea at Lowick when he is on his way from Tipton to the county town. This can only mean that Lowick was accessible from, if not actually on, the Coventry to Warwick road. Now, both this, and the distance would suit Stivichall better, and the fact that the railway was to run through Lowick parish does actually exclude Baginton, if the identification is to be a strict one. But the description of the manor house in its relation to the church, and to the parsonage, and the point about the compact village with its twin cottages, fits Baginton too well to be overlooked. It may be that Lowick is a combination of the two, and that here, as with so much else in *Middlemarch*, a cut and dried identification is impossible.

Tipton and Freshitt are five miles away from Lowick, either by coach, or by walking across Halsell Common. Orienting George Eliot's diagram on Middlemarch as Coventry, and on Lowick identified as either Stivichall or Baginton, Tipton and Freshitt would seem to be Keresley and Coundon. But Keresley and Coundon were not weaving villages, and Tipton and Freshitt, five miles from Lowick, and three from Middlemarch, can perhaps be identified, as Foleshill and Exhall.

The *Quarry* proves that George Eliot took care to make her story conform to the course of the Reform Bill, and contains the dates of the university terms at Oxford and Cambridge for Fred Vincy's examination.

George Eliot's accuracy in persons and events is not great enough for the historian to accept her evidence as the literal truth. But, then, it is not this sort of evidence that the historian wants from *Middlemarch*. This great novel is valuable as a picture of society, and of the relations of classes, of the spread of scandal, and of fashion. It does not matter whether one can identify in Mr. Vincy an actual ribbon-manufacturer, provided that Mr. Vincy himself is not an improbable one. Nor does it matter whether Mr. Bulstrode is an actual banker, Mr. Brooke and Sir James Chettam actual landlords, or Lydgate an actual doctor. Each of them stands for a class, and it is the way they talk about and behave to each other that matters to the historian. If one agrees that George Eliot had the skill and opportunity to portray this kind of historical fact, then one may safely infer that in *Middlemarch* George Eliot has laid a large part of Coventry society bare to the roots.

INDEX

Acts of Parliament, ix, 21, 23-24, 25, 26, 28, 29, 34, 37, 38, 40, 41, 56, 57, 92, 93, 95, 134

Acton, Lord, 9

Agricultural villages, 1, 11, 45, 72

Agriculture, healthy occupation, 107-12

Albutt, Dr., of Leeds, 143

Allotments and gardens, 23, 26, 41, 70, 75, 84, 85, 86, 101, 108, 110-11

Andrews, Anne, 104

Andrews, William, 1; diary, 16, 122; apprentice, 16; character, 16; visits Great Exhibition, 16; Paris, 16; employed by Cash's, 16; appointed manager, 104-5; watches cottage factories being built, 102, 104-6; signs list of prices, 119; works in Switzerland, 78, 131; re-engaged by Cash's, 131-2; records failure of cottage factories, 131-2

Anglo-French Treaty of 1860, 119-22, 124

Ansty, 19 note 1, 45

Apprentices, 1, 13, 13 note 4, 15, 16, 17, 28, 51, 64-65, 87-88, 104; see also Freemen

Arbury, 1

Asthill, 19 note 1

Baginton, 104, 144

Baker, Robert, H.M. Factory Inspector, 95-99, 110, 128-9, 133-5

Banbury, Thomas, 34, 36

Banking, 11, 25, 36, 57, 123, 128, 145; see also Savings Bank

Barnwell, Mr. Stephen, 93, 94

Barracks, 33

Basle, 43, 128, 131

Beck, Mr., 30, 36, 48, 60, 139

Bedworth, 45, 49, 129

Biggin, 19 note 1

Bird Grove, 4

Birmingham, 19, 20, 21, 25, 78, 110, 130, 131, 139

Blackburn, 130

Boston, Lord, 23

Bray, Caroline, 4-5, 108

Bray, Charles, 1; early life and marriage, 4-5; entertains at Rosehill, 5, 77; meets and influences George Eliot, 5-9; recognizes himself in *Middlemarch*, 5, 143; philosophy of, 6-7; Gutteridge on, 15; philosophy vindicated, 18, 80; always happy, 12;

Christianity harmful, 9; founds co-operative society, 10, 107-8; ribbon manufacturer, 10, 62; in local politics, 10, 12, 40; collects statistics for Joseph Fletcher, 43 note 2; writings, 11-12; views on Gladstone and Liberal Party, 14-15; on cottage factories, 11, 99, 106-12, 125

Bray, Charles, of Earl Street, 62

Brewers, 24

Brickmakers, 67

British Association, 11, 109

Browett, William, 34, 36

Brown, Mr. Henry, 94

Brown, Mr. T., 90

Brown and Thomas, Messrs., 126

Brussels, 131

Buckley, Mr. Nathaniel, 90

Bubbenhall, 104

Buckingham, James Silk, 109

Bulkington, 45, 129

Burbury, Thomas, 30, 48

Burdett, Sir Francis, 30

Burgesses, 34-35

Bury, Dr., 143

Caldicott, Mr., 36, 89, 90, 126

Caludon, 19 note 1

Cambridge University, 101, 144

Capitalization of ribbon trade, 17, 17 note 1, 49, 50, 106, 139

Carpenters, 72

Carter, Mr., Town Clerk, 32, 36-37

Cash's, 16-17, 83, 101, 102, 104-6, 107-8, 111, 122, 131-3

Castle Inn, 55

Cemetery, 30 note 2, 37-38

Chapelfields, 23, 41, 82-85

Chapman, James, 128-9

Charities, 17 note 1, 23, 28, 34, 35, 41

Chartism, 11, 139

Cheylesmore Park, 21, 41

Children's employment, 46, 64-65, 66, 109, 133-4

Chilvers Coton, 45, 129

Cholera, 69

Clarke, Edward, surgeon, of Meriden, 143

Class consciousness, x, xi, 11, 14, 28, 35-36, 41-42, 52-53, 57, 68, 71, 76, 79-80, 83, 85, 87, 88, 91-92, 95, 106-7, 114, 116, 122-9, 134-5, 138-9

Clubs, 67, 73

Cobden Treaty, *see* Anglo-French Treaty
Coal and colliers, 1, 19, 20, 64-65, 67, 76, 108
Coleman, Mr., 90
Cologne, 131
Combe Abbey, 31
Combe, George, phrenologist, 5, 9
Combination Laws, 57
Common-land, 21, 23, 128; *see also* Gosford Green, Greyfriars Green
Commons, House of, 28, 30, 36, 37, 119
Congleton, 43
Connolly, Dr., reformer, 5
Co-operation, 106, 107 note 3, 110-11, 134
Co-operative Society, 10, 108
Cope, Mr., 49, 51, 55, 89
Corn Exchange, 125
Corn Laws, 31
Cottage factories, in Hillfields, 42; origins of, 94-96; records of, 96-98; number and location of, 99; arrangement of, 99-101, 109-10; Bray and the theory of, 11, 106-12; Cash's build, 16-17, 102, 104-6; failure of, 132-3; Eli Green's block of sixty-seven in Hillfields, 102; struggle with factories, 94-95, 110, 114-18, 121; failure of, 132-5
Coundon, 108, 144
Coventry, ix-xi; as a provincial centre, 1, 19; described by Charles Bray, 12; described in *Middlemarch*, 11, 143-5; size of, 25, 57; population of, 24, 25-26, 28, 39, 80, 87, 129-30; surrounded by pasture lands, 21-24; railway, 20; streets, 24, 26, 32, 33, 38, 41, 57, 102; markets, 24; cemetery, 30 note 2, 37; water supply, 26, 38, 72; sewerage, 26, 38; houses, 24, 25-26, 38-39, 41-42, 67, 73-75, 82-87; compared with Nottingham and Leicester, 137-9
Coventry Canal, 1, 104
Coventry City Council, 10, 34-36, 37-38, 40, 52, 93; elections for, 35.
Coventry constituency, Parliamentary elections, 19, 25, 26-31, 37, 52, 76, 78, 143-4
Coventry Corporation, 10, 29, 32-34, 35-36, 52
Coventry, county of, 19, 37, 45
Coventry Herald, 10, 11, 12, 61-62, 109, 115-16, 143
Coventry Labourers and Artisans Friendly Society, 107-8
Coventry Labour Protection Society, 90
Coventry Mercury, 61
Coventry Mutual Improvement Society, 15

Coventry Standard, 10, 31, 43 note 2, 51, 61-62, 116, 122, 126
Craven, Earl of, 31, 36
Craven Arms, 91

Dalton and Barton, Messrs., 132
Dawson, George, preacher, 5
Day, Mr., 49, 66 note 2, 94, 116
Derby, 43, 44, 48, 49, 92, 137, 138
Design, School of, 120
Dewes, Mr. Henry, 94
Dissent, 1, 139
Domestic Service, 71, 85, 86
Donkeying, 48, 60, 92
Drapers Fields, 106, 119
Dresser, Mr., 90
Dresser, Mrs., 15, 67
Dyeing and dyers, 17, 24, 44, 46, 76

Earlsdon, 41
Eaves, Mr. William, 94
Eld, George, 36
Elections to Parliament, *see* Coventry constituency
Eliot, George, ix; early life, 1, 3-4; meets Bray, 5-6; influenced by Bray, 6-9; philosophy of, 8-9; vindicated, 18, 80; Middlemarch as Coventry, 10-11, 143-5; *see also Middlemarch, Scenes of Clerical Life, The Mill on the Floss*
Ellice, Edward, M.P., 30, 57, 119
Emerson, philosopher, 5
Emigration, 130-1
Employers, *see* Masters
Enclosure, 40-41
Evans, Christiana, 143
Evans, Mary Ann, *see* Eliot, George
Evans, Robert, 1, 3, 4, 6, 143
Exhall, 19 note 1, 45, 70, 129, 144

Factory Acts, 92, 95, 134
Factories, x, 15, 24, 30, 42, 45-46, 48, 49, 52-53, 58, 60, 66-67, 68, 75, 76, 79, 80, 84, 88, 91, 92, 93-95, 109, 110, 113-18, 126, 133, 134, 139
Factory Inspector, *see* Baker, Robert
Far East, 44
Fay, C. R., historian, 71
Felix Holt, 1, 144
Fielden, John, 56
Fletcher, Joseph, Assistant Commissioner to Unemployed Handloom Weavers Commission, 43 note 2, 49, 64, 72, 114
Foleshill, 19 note 1, 45, 49, 65, 97, 99, 117, 124, 129, 144
Food, price of, 70, 113

France, and the French, 31, 43, 44, 111, 119-22, 124, 131; *see also* Lyons, Paris, St. Etienne
Franklin, the Misses' School, 3
Franklin, Messrs., 126
Freemen, 13-14, 19, 21, 23, 24, 26-31, 32, 34-35, 36, 39-42, 52, 58, 69, 72, 82, 87-88; *see also* Apprentices
Free Trade, 30-31, 43, 119-21, 137

Gardens, *see* Allotments
Germany, 111
Gilbert, Mr. S. I., 94
Gladstone, W. E., 14, 15, 119-22
Godiva, Countess, 19, 128 note 4
Godiva Procession, 25, 78
Goode, Mr., 59, 90
Gosford, 23, 93, 94
Gosford Green, 25
Government, the, *see* Westminster
Greatorex, Mr., Inspector for Local Board of Health, 38, 93, 97
Green, Mr. Eli, 102, 104, 106, 111, 129
Greenway, Mr. W. R., 98
Greyfriars Green, 60, 89, 127
Griff, 20
Gutteridge, Joseph, 1; apprentice, 13, 28; youth, 15, 76-77; independence of, 14, 68; engagement and marriage, 13, 15, 17, 77; love of birds, flowers, fossils, 16, 53, 76-77; his museum, 16; sees Mr. Beck's factory burned down, 48; and Bray, 15; and Gladstone, 14, 121; in 1860-61, 129; at Paris Exhibition, 15

Hall, George, 114, 122
Hammerton, Mr. S., 94
Harmony Hall, 106
Harnall, 19 note 1
Hart, Mr., 91, 94, 115, 117
Hart, Mr. James, 126
Hartshill, 45
Haymes, Mr., 62
Health, Local Board of, 35, 38-39, 42, 93, 93 note 4, 96-99, 102; *see also* Greatorex, Mr.
Heathcoat, inventor of lace machine, 138
Hemming, Mr. George, 98
Henley-le-Wood-End, 19 note 1
Hennell, Caroline, *see* Bray, Caroline
Hennell, Charles, 5
Hennell, Mary, 107 note 3
Hennell, Mr., 89
Hill and Hollow Close, 58
Hillfields, 23, 38, 41, 42, 73, 75, 76, 80, 82, 83, 97, 99, 108, 110
Hinckley, 130
Hobbes, Thomas, 140-1
Holyhead Road, 19-21, 24, 25, 39

Holy Trinity Church, 24
Horwell, 19 note 1
Hosiery Trade, 44, 137-8
Hospitals, 143

Iliffe, Peters, and Hamer, Messrs., 115
Inchley, William, 98
Industrial disputes, 12, 33-34, 42, 45, 49, 54-63, 68, 88-93, 113-19, 123-7, 138
Isle of Man, 104
Italy, 44

Jenkins, Mr. J., 52
Jephcott, Mr., 90, 114
J. L., of Foleshill, 124-5

Kenilworth, 130
Keresley, 19 note 1, 144
Kidderminster, 62
Kingfield, 16, 101, 102, 104-6, 110, 132, 133

Labour Party, 15, 139
Laisser-Faire, 15, 42, 62-63; *see also* Free Trade, List of Prices
Lammas and Michaelmas Lands, ix, 21-24, 29, 32, 39-41, 57, 76, 107; *see also* Common-land
Lancashire, 130
Landlords, 45, 107, 129, 139, 145
Leamington, 130
Lee, Mr. James, 97
Leek, 43, 137
Leicester, 25, 109, 130, 131, 137-9
Leicestershire, 44
Leigh, Lord, 31, 128
Liberalism, Liberal Party, Liberals and Radicals, 10, 13-15, 29-31, 35-37, 80, 120, 122, 139
Lilley, Mr. Charles, 57
List of Prices, ix, x, 15, 17-18, 45, 53-63, 66, 69, 79-80, 81, 88-93, 95, 113, 115, 121, 123-7, 129, 131, 137-9
Locke, John, 140-1
London, 4, 19, 20, 28 note 5, 44, 49, 50, 104
Looms, 15, 15 note 3, 44, 46, 52, 53, 54, 68, 80, 113-14; application of power to, 46, 48-49, 93, 95-99, 101, 102, 109-10, 113, 133; Dutch engine loom, 47, 49, 60, 66, 70; single hand loom, 46-49, 60, 64; Jacquard loom, 47-49, 66, 70
Lords, House of, 29-30, 36
Luddism, 139
Lyons, 43, 131

Macclesfield, 43, 72, 137, 138

Magistrates, 33, 34, 48, 52, 57, 59, 60, 79, 80, 90, 91, 117, 124, 139
Mainz, 131
Malthus, 109
Manchester, 43, 44, 57, 64, 114, 137, 139
Manufacturers, *see* Masters
Marx, Karl, 134
Masters, in ribbon trade, 49-52; old masters, 12, 35-36, 49-52, 79, 140; new masters or small masters, x, 17, 36, 50-52, 53, 54, 56, 62, 79, 80; honourable or good masters, 54-55, 58, 61, 62, 79, 88, 126, 140-1; dishonourable or bad masters, 54-55, 61-62, 63, 88, 140-1; masters and weavers, ix, 34, 45-46, 48-49, 51-52, 53-63, 68, 69, 79, 85-87, 88-93, 104, 106, 110-11, 113-19, 120, 121, 122-8, 131-2, 140-1; rival masters, *see* France, Switzerland, Derby; *see also* Andrews, William and Bray, Charles, Cash's
Mayor, 32, 33, 35, 36, 37, 58-59, 69, 80, 89, 90, 117, 122
Melbourne, Lord, 30
Members of Parliament, 28, 29, 30, 30 note 2, 119
Merridew, Mr., 89
Michaelmas Lands, *see* Lammas Lands
Middlemarch, 3, 5, 8, 10, 11, 20, 33, 36, 49, 51, 61, 73, 78, 143-5
Mill on the Floss, 3
Moore, Mr. James, 98

Napoleon III, 119
Napoleonic Wars, 50, 55, 56, 76, 77, 140
Newcastle, Duke of, 138
Newdegate, 20
Nottingham, 26, 137-9
Nuneaton, 1, 45, 47, 49, 64, 129, 144

Odell, Mr., 94
Ordnance Survey, 26, 38, 93, 93 note 4, 99
Oxford University, 101, 144
Owen, Robert, 7, 106, 107, 125

Palmerston, 120
Paris, 15, 16, 104, 131
Paxton, Joseph, 30 note 2, 37
Peel, Sir Robert, 31, 70
Phrenology, 4, 5, 9, 14
Pinley, 19 note 1
Police, 33, 60, 92, 117, 124
Pollard, Mr. E. J., memoirs, 99, 101, 101 note 2
Pollard, Mr., 61
Poor rates, 37, 45, 138
Poor relief, 28, 53-54, 64, 68-69, 124; *see also* Relief funds

Pridmore, Mr., 117-18
Primrose Hill, 76-77
Protection, 30-31, 43, 120-1, 125, 127
Public houses, gin shops, 20, 55, 58, 71, 72-73, 79, 89, 91; Castle Inn, 55; Craven Arms, 91
Public opinion, ix, 11, 17, 34, 42, 61-62, 71, 80, 81, 88, 89, 92, 116, 118, 138, 139, 140

Radford, 19 note 1
Railway, London to Birmingham, 20, 24, 39
Ratliff, Mr., 36, 90, 92, 116
Read, Mr., 114
Read, Mr. T., 126, 133
Reform, of House of Commons, 29, 65; of Municipal Corporation, 32, 34-37
Relief funds, 69-70, 122-3, 128
Religion, 4, 9, 15, 69, 77, 125, 127
Ribbon trade, origin of, 44; European towns engaged in, 43; English towns engaged in, 43; local villages engaged in, 44-45; markets of, 43, 121-2; fluctuation of, 44, 67-68; fashion and, 44, 121; raw material for, 44; preparation of raw materials, 46; wages for, 66-67; weaving and looms, 46-49; classes engaged in, the masters, 49-52, men, 52-53; regulation of wages, 53-63; transformation of, x, xi, summarized, 79-80; effect of watch trade on, 81, 87-88; changing nature of struggle to maintain list of prices, 88-93; growth of factory system, 93-95, 113; growth of cottage factory system, 94-99; factory and cottage factory in conflict, 113-19; Anglo-French commercial treaty, 119-22; weavers' delegations to France and Switzerland, 121, 131; effect of Treaty, 122; great strike of 1860, 123-7, consequences of, 127-8; relief of distress, 128-9; emigration of weavers, 129-31; end of cottage factories, 133-5; compared with hosiery trade, 137-8; *see also* Cottage factories, Factories, Industrial disputes, List of prices, Looms, Masters, Steam power, Trades unions, Undertakers, Unemployment, Wages, Weavers
Robinson and Lynes, Messrs., 92
Rosehill, 5, 10, 17, 62, 143
Rugby, 130
Rutland, Duke of, 138
Ryley, Mr., 90
Ryton Bridge, 104

St. Etienne, 43, 67, 128, 131

St. Mary's Hall, 69, 91
St. Michael's Church and Vicar, 5, 24, 77, 125, 127
St. Peter's Church, 76
Savings Bank, 73
Scenes of Clerical Life, 3 note 1, 71 note 1
Schooling, 15, 65
Scotland, 104
Sewerage, 26, 38
Sheffield, 125
Sherbourne, river, 23, 24, 37
Sherbourne House, 83
Shilton, 45
Shopkeepers, 10, 11, 25, 58, 79, 80, 124, 126
Sibree, Mrs., 5
Silk, *see* Ribbon trade, raw material of
Simons, H., grocer, 70
Simpson, James, 5
Smith, Adam, 141
Smith, Mr. Samuel, 98
Smith, William, 98
Soden, Mr. T., 129
Soldiers, 33, 48
Sowe, 19 note 1, 45, 129
Spark, Benjamin, 30, 48
Spencer, Herbert, 5
Spencer, Mr. William, 94
Spencer and Horsfall, Messrs., 90
Spitalfields, 43, 72, 137, 138
Spitalfields Act, 56, 56 note 2
Spon End, 24, 25, 38, 41
Steam power, x, 45, 46, 48-49, 93, 94-96, 101, 102, 109-10, 113, 133-4, 137, 139, 140
Stivichall, 19 note 1, 144
Stoke, 19 note 1, 23, 83, 129
Stoneleigh, 31, 104
Stonemasons, 72
Stratford, 130
Streets: Adelaide Street, 101; Albert Street, 98, 99, 101; Allesley Old Road, no. 61 described, 85-87; Berry Street, 97, 99, 101, 102; Bradford Street, 99; Brick Kiln Lane, 108; Broadgate, 97; Brook Street, 97, 101, 102; Cash's Lane, 104; Castle Street, Hillfields, no. 20 described, 73, 75; Cox Street, 94; Craven Street, no. 34 described, 83; Earl Street, 25, 62, 94, 97; Edgewick Road, 97; Far Gosford Street, 25; Fleet Street, 25; Ford Street, 37; Gilbert Street, 98, 99; Gosford Street, 25; Hertford Street, 25; Hertford Square, 101 note 2; High Street, 25; Hill Street, 94, 108; Jordan Well, 25; King Street, 94, 98; Lancasterian Yard, 94; London Road, 37, 108; Lower

Ford Street, 37, 128; Much Park Street, 10, 61, 62, 94; Paynes Lane, 98, 99; Queen Street, 98, 99, no. 32 described, 85-87; St. Agnes Lane, 15; Smithford Street, 25, 33; Spon Street, 24, 25, 61; Stoney Stanton Road, 98; Vernon Street, 39, 97, 101, 102, no. 11 described, 75; Warwick Row, 24; Weston Street, 98; West Orchard, 94; White Friars Lane, 94; Yardley Street, 16, 39
Strikes, *see* Industrial disputes
Switzerland and the Swiss, 31, 43, 78, 124, 131

Tariffs, *see* Protection
Telford, Thomas, 19
The Times, 123
Thomas, Mr., 61
Topshops, 75, 96, 101 note 2, 106, 109
Tories, Tory Party, 10, 30-31, 35, 80
Townsend, Mr., 94
Toynbee, Arnold, historian, 139
Trade-cycle, 67-68, 111
Trades unions: weavers' unions and committees, 15, 25, 56-60, 63, 80, 88-93, 116-18, 123-7, 140; manufacturers unite with weavers, 57; manufacturers' associations, 60-61, 79, 118
Troughton's Bank, 57
Turkey, 44

Undertakers in the ribbon trade, 49-50, 64-65, 137
Unemployed Handloom Weavers Commission, *see* Fletcher, Joseph
Unemployment, x, 14, 25, 33, 44-45, 54, 67-69, 78, 107, 111-12, 122, 127-8, 131
United States of America, 121, 130, 131

Vales, the, 36
Victoria, Queen, 128

Wages in ribbon trade, 50, 64-65, 66-67, 72, 81, 113; piece rates, 113-16, 118; weekly wages, 79, 113-18; *see also* List of prices
Walsgrave on Sowe, *see* Sowe
Warwick, 130
Watch manufacture, ix, x, 24, 28, 36, 41, 72; origins of, 81; organization of, 81-82; no list of prices, 81; superiority of, 82-83; standards of living and houses in, 82-87; proximity of masters and men, 83-84, 87; drift of freemen to, 87-88, 114
Waterloo, 131

Water supply, 26, 38

Weavers, classes of, 52-53; class divisions among, x, 42, 79-80, 93, 116-17, 126; better class of, x, 41-42, 114; lower class of, x, 42, 68, 95; first-hand journeymen, 52, 53, 58, 66, 68, 72, 75, 76, 79, 80, 88, 94, 95, 101, 114, 134; journeymen's journeymen, 52, 53, 66, 75, 76, 79; outdoor weavers, 45, 52, 66, 67, 68, 80, 88, 91, 93, 94-95, 96, 102, 113-18, 126, 134-5; factory weavers, see Factories; country weavers, 1, 11, 44-45, 47, 50, 63, 64-65, 68, 70-71, 72, 76, 79, 114, 118, 127, 137; honourable or good weavers, 54-55, 61, 63, 79, 88, 140-1; dishonourable or bad weavers, 54-55, 61, 63, 88, 140-1; hours of work, 64-65, 67; wages, see Wages; food of, 70, 72; housing of, 53, 68, 70-71, 73-75, see also 82-87; health of, 71, 73, 75-76; sickness clubs, 72-73; recreations, 76-78, 104; standards of living summarized, 75; did not go to church, 77; census of, 43 note 2; see also Gutteridge, Joseph, Masters and weavers

Westminster, government at, x, 31, 52-53, 56, 71, 119-21, 125, 141

Whigs, see Liberalism

Whitbread, Samuel, 30

Whitley, 19 note 1

Whitwells, the, 36

Whoberley, 19 note 1

Widdrington, Rev. S. H., 125, 127

Wilmot, W., solicitor, 91

Women's work, 11, 28, 44, 46, 47, 51, 52, 53, 64-65, 71, 81, 109, 116

Worcester, Mr., 90

Wyken, 19 note 1